Letort Paper

THE AFGHANISTAN QUESTION
AND THE RESET IN U.S.-RUSSIAN RELATIONS

Richard J. Krickus

October 2011

*****

*****

Comments pertaining to this report are invited and should be forwarded to: Director, Strategic Studies Institute, U.S. Army War College, 632 Wright Ave, Carlisle, PA 17013-5046.

*****

Published by Books Express Publishing
Books Express Publishing, 2011
ISBN 978-1-78039-986-7

Books Express publications are available from all good retail and online booksellers. For publishing proposals and direct ordering please contact us at: info@books-express.com

FOREWORD

Defense Secretary Robert Gates has observed that the ability of the United States and Russia to cooperate in Afghanistan represents a solid test of their reset in relations. Skeptics in Washington and Moscow, however, scoff at the idea. In the first case, critics cite the awesome value gap that separates the two sides as well as compelling evidence that the Kremlin is bent on a course of confrontation and not cooperation with the West — witness the 2008 Russian-Georgian War. In the second one, Russian critics claim that there is no justification for Moscow to help Washington in what many Kremlin overlords believe is a losing cause. Moreover, Obama says the right things but, like his predecessor, he ignores Russian concerns about the Afghanistan Question — such as curtailing the flow of deadly heroin to the cities of Russia.

Without dismissing the barriers to cooperation, American statesmen like Henry Kissinger and George Shultz claim that Russia's help should be welcomed in dealing with the global jihadist threat, nuclear proliferation, and climate change. In keeping with efforts on the part of past administrations to advance common interests with regimes that may adhere to different values, the Obama administration has pursued limited security cooperation with Russia much as Presidents Richard Nixon and Ronald Reagan did decades ago.

In turn, Russian strategists fear that should the Americans fail in Afghanistan, their former Central Asian Republics will fall to militant Islamists. At the same time, emboldened by the West's setback in Afghanistan, al-Qaeda and affiliated terrorist organizations will support their brethren in the Northern Caucasus who are waging war against the Russian infidels and launching terrorist attacks within Russia proper. Taken together, these actions threaten the Kremlin's "20-20 Modernization" drive that Prime Minister Vladimir Putin deems to be Russia's greatest security priority.

In this monograph, Dr. Richard Krickus provides the historical background to the Afghanistan Question and assesses current events in the Afghan war with three objectives in mind:

1. To determine whether Russian-American cooperation in Afghanistan has been successful. Toward this end, he revisits the rationale behind the Soviet invasion of Afghanistan 30 years ago; shows how it and the civil war that followed it helped give rise to al-Qaeda and the Taliban; and assesses the failure of authorities in Washington and Moscow to prevent an evil partnership that led to September 11, 2001 (9/11).

2. To identify and evaluate the successes and failures of the counterinsurgency (COIN) strategy as the transition from U.S. to Afghanistan authority gains traction in the 2011-14 time frame. Among other things, he considers three scenarios that characterize current operations in Afghanistan and assesses two plausible alternative outcomes. He claims that while the goals of COIN have not been fully realized, the capacity of al-Qaeda in Afghanistan has been dismantled for all intents and purposes, and, through our counterterrorist operations, the Taliban have experienced serious reversals. Successes against the Taliban, however, remain fragile, and the road ahead is a difficult one.

3. To provide conclusions and recommendations bearing on developments in Afghanistan, Dr. Krickus submits a number of provocative observations and policy preferences in anticipating the difficult withdrawal of U.S. troops from Afghanistan. Among other

things, he proposes that the road to a successful resolution of the Afghanistan conflict must include political reconciliation with the Taliban through a diplomatic initiative — Bonn II — that enlists the support of all major stakeholders in the region. At the same time, Pakistan must be put on notice that it cannot continue to provide sanctuaries to jihadists that are killing Americans without consequences. Looking forward, the U.S. military must maintain its capacity to address jihadist threats to American and allied security by adopting appropriate counterterrorist policies. Furthermore, given dramatic changes in the international security environment — as exemplified by new influential actors like Brazil, China, and India — and its own daunting domestic economic problems, the United States must reduce its profile in the Greater Middle East.

In sum, he concludes that, while modest, Russia's help in advancing the goals of the United States in the Afghan War has been important. Today, for example, with Moscow's assistance, more than 50 percent of the cargo that is provided to U.S. fighting forces transits through the Northern Distribution Network (NDN). As U.S. troops exit from the country, the NDN will acquire even greater logistical significance.

Given the record of modest success in Afghanistan, the United States should expand its joint ventures with Moscow in a common front against jihadist terrorist groups. They should continue as long as the vital interests of the United States are served.

DOUGLAS C. LOVELACE, JR.
Director
Strategic Studies Institute

ABOUT THE AUTHOR

RICHARD J. KRICKUS is a Distinguished Professor Emeritus at the University of Mary Washington and has held the Oppenheimer Chair for Warfighting Strategy at the U.S. Marine Corps University. Previously he cofounded The National Center for Urban Ethnic Affairs in Washington, DC, and in the early 1970s began conducting research on the Union of Soviet Socialist Republics' "nationalities question." In this connection, he began to write about popular unrest among the people of Lithuania. In 1990, Sajudis, the Lithuanian popular front movement, invited him to serve as an international monitor for the first democratic election conducted in Soviet Lithuania. Dr. Krickus has offered testimony to the Senate Foreign Relations Committee and has lectured at the U.S. Foreign Service Institute, the Polish Foreign Ministry, the European Commission, and other domestic and foreign venues on the Soviet Union/Russia, the Baltic countries, NATO, and Kaliningrad. He has published widely on these issues for academic and policy-oriented journals as well as various newspapers, including *The Washington Post*, *The Chicago Sun-Times*, *The Los Angeles Times*, and *The Wall Street Journal Europe*. For 8 years Dr. Krickus wrote a column on world affairs for *Lietuvos Rytas*, Lithuania's leading national daily. He has appeared as a commentator on Soviet-Russian affairs on U.S. radio and television on numerous occasions. He is the author of a number of books, including: *Pursuing the American Dream*; *The Superpowers in Crisis*; *Showdown: The Lithuanian Rebellion and the Break-Up of the Soviet Empire*; *The Kaliningrad Question*; *Iron Troikas: The New Threat from the East*; and *Medvedev's Plan: Giving Russia a Voice but Not a Veto in a New European Security System*. Dr. Krickus holds a B.A. in government from the College of William and Mary, an M.A. in international affairs from the University of Massachusetts, and a Ph.D. in comparative politics from Georgetown University.

SUMMARY

U.S. Defense Secretary Robert M. Gates has said that the ability of the United States and Russia to cooperate in Afghanistan will be a solid test of their reset in relations. That proposition is the thesis of this monograph. Many analysts in both countries would agree with this assessment, but a significant number of them believe a fruitful reset is implausible.

American skeptics argue that under Vladimir Putin, Russia has reversed the timid efforts that Boris Yeltsin embraced to safeguard political pluralism in Russia. But in addition to the awesome value gap that compromises cooperation, Russia has demonstrated that it favors confrontation and not cooperation with the West; witness the 2008 Russia-Georgian War.

From the Russian perspective, one finds similar arguments against cooperation. For example, the Americans are looking to exit from a military engagement that is not going well for them, and all metrics suggest things will get worse instead of better. Why, then, should Russia become involved in a lost cause? The Americans want Russia's help because the U.S. population has turned against the war in Afghanistan and in 2012 most European troops will leave Afghanistan.

Without discounting the many roadblocks, leaders in both countries believe that even limited security cooperation is in their vital interest. In this connection, both Washington and Moscow deem a return of the Taliban in Afghanistan as detrimental to their respective security priorities.

In the U.S. case, should terrorist bases be resurrected in Afghanistan, American citizens run the risk of becoming victims in a repeat of September 11, 2001 (9/11). To prevent this ominous outcome, the United

States has embarked upon military operations in co-operation with North Atlantic Treaty Organization (NATO) and Afghan forces. The coalition has received limited but significant assistance from Russia in the areas of arms, diplomacy, intelligence, logistics, and training.

Likewise, Russia has a number of incentives to help the U.S.-led coalition in Afghanistan: curtailing the flow of drugs from that country to Russia; protecting the Central Asian states that are integral to Russia's economic prosperity; and denying jihadists the opportunity to conduct terrorist operations in the North Caucasus and Russia proper. In truth, Russia has more to lose than the United States should the coalition stumble in Afghanistan.

It is the purpose of this paper to evaluate the existing status of U.S.-Russian cooperation and the prospects for future joint security ventures in the region. In the process, a second related major rationale will be to assess the coalition's successes and failures in meeting the jihadist threat in Afghanistan.

To put the Afghanistan Question in perspective, the 1979 Soviet invasion of Afghanistan will be assessed along with the U.S. reaction to it, and subsequent events like the civil war that followed the collapse of the communist government in Kabul, the rise of the Taliban, and its association with al-Qaeda that led to the 9/11 strikes on the Twin Towers and the Pentagon.

Special attention will be devoted to the support that Russia provided the United States in the wake of 9/11 and, more recently, its role in advancing U.S. goals in America's "longest war." Toward this end, the performance of the Obama administration's counterinsurgency (COIN) operations will be explored through three scenarios.

The first (Plan A) involves current facts on the ground followed by two plausible alternative scenarios: Partition of Afghanistan (Plan B, popularized by the former U.S. Ambassador to India, Robert Blackwill), and the third or worst-case scenario I (Plan C), involves returning the Taliban to power.

It is against this backdrop that conclusions and recommendations bearing on the future of U.S. activities in Afghanistan will be considered. For example:

- The time has come to acknowledge that what has been mislabeled the "global war on terrorism" may better be labeled a "civil war within Islam." The United States can influence that monumental historical development only at the margins.
- Given the changing international environment and profound economic challenges at home, U.S. authorities should advance existing efforts to reconcile with the Taliban. This undertaking will be a component of a larger diplomatic effort (Bonn II) that includes stakeholders in the region such as China, India, Pakistan, and perhaps even Iran along with the Central Asian states, Russia, and Saudi Arabia.
- As concern about personnel security surges, so will pressure from the American public to significantly reduce the military budget and reassess U.S. priorities in the Greater Middle East.
- Many strategists believe the current level of military operations is unsustainable and is not justified by the jihadist threat. It can be adequately met through counterterrorist operations that have proven to be successful in marginalizing the jihadists in Afghanistan.

- As the U.S. presidential election approaches, public concern about the duplicity of allies like Pakistan will compel U.S. leaders to demand that Islamabad deny sanctuary to jihadists who are killing Americans or face the consequences.
- The United States will be required to engage in multilateral security efforts with countries that may not share its values—such as Russia—but have common security problems. This enterprise has been characterized by some analysts as the "Obama Doctrine."
- Russian cooperation in Afghanistan, although limited, has been significant as exemplified by the fact that by the end of 2011, more than 50 percent of the cargo required by our fighting forces there will transit through the Northern Distribution Network—made possible by Russia's cooperation.

The U.S.-Russian reset will continue to face challenges; for example, it could be subverted by a new round of Russia-Georgia enmity, and differences over the U.S. missile defense system in Europe could result in a split between the two sides. But as long as security cooperation promotes U.S. national interests, it should continue. Finally, in considering what may be deemed controversial conclusions and recommendations, the words of Defense Secretary Gates come to mind. In his last policy speech before his counterparts at the June 2011 NATO Summit, he said, ". . . true friends occasionally must speak bluntly with one another for the sake of those greater interests and values that bind us together."

THE AFGHANISTAN QUESTION
AND THE RESET IN U.S.-RUSSIAN RELATIONS

INTRODUCTION

Former U.S. Defense Secretary Robert M. Gates has suggested that the ability of the United States and Russia to cooperate in Afghanistan will be a solid test of their reset in relations. That is the thesis of this monograph. Many analysts in both countries would agree with this assessment, but a significant number of them believe a fruitful reset is implausible.

The American Skeptics.

U.S. critics assert that a prominent value gap diminishes significant long-term cooperation. Under Vladimir Putin's rule, the tepid steps toward democracy taken by Boris Yeltsin have been reversed. Political opponents have been silenced or arrested, there is no widespread news media freedom, the courts have been compromised, and the government has been complicit in allowing corrupt officials and criminal organizations to flourish. In sum, the fine words of President Dmitry Medvedev aside, autocracy, not pluralism, has been the hallmark of Putin's Russia ever since he and his colleagues in the Russian secret police (KGB) entered the Kremlin.

Internationally, Putin has matched his tough rhetoric with harsh actions. Moscow has exploited its hydrocarbon wealth to punish governments in the former Soviet space that resist its aggressive efforts to influence their economic and political affairs. In the process, the Kremlin has exploited gas and oil price spikes, pipeline disruptions, down-stream investments, and even cyber-attacks. What is more, neighbors have been unsettled by military doctrine that pledges to defend Russians living abroad. Worst of all, the 2008 Russian invasion of Georgia and the wresting of territory from the Tbilisi government demonstrate that the Kremlin overlords will use brute force to accomplish their objectives. Russia's invasion of Georgia signifies the Kremlin's true intentions and suggests confrontation, not cooperation.

Initiatives like Medvedev's call for a new European security system are designed to undermine the North Atlantic Treaty Organization (NATO) and to divide its members. At times, the Kremlin may engage in ad hoc security cooperation such as in Afghanistan, but on its terms. Whatever short-term tactical advantages are secured through the reset campaign will ultimately result in a strategic liability for the United States and its allies.

Russian Skeptics.

From the Russian perspective, one finds similar arguments against cooperation. For example, the Americans are looking to exit from a military engagement that is not going well for them, and all metrics suggest things will get worse instead of better. Why, then, should Russia become involved in a lost cause? The Americans want Russia's help because their own population has turned against the war in Afghanistan, and most European troops will be out of the country by late 2012. As a consequence, they are desperately reaching out for helpmates. But while Washington welcomes Moscow's assistance in arms transfers, development, diplomacy, intelligence, logistics, and training, it has categorically refused to end poppy production and the shipment of heroin to Russia. In sum, it refuses to acknowledge one of Russia's major incentives for denying the Taliban a victory in Afghanistan. As is typically the case, the Americans ask for concessions but in turn are grudging in giving anything back to Russia. Rhetoric aside, Barack Obama, like George Bush, has demonstrated that it is "his way or the highway." Clearly, American hubris is alive and well no matter who occupies the White House.

One more thing: in the improbable event of a U.S. victory in Afghanistan, Washington will seek permanent bases in Greater Central Asia. This outcome fits perfectly with the intent of Pentagon planners to encircle Russia and impose upon it a geo-strategic environment favorable to the United States.

While there are ample reasons to view a reset in U.S.-Russian relations with skepticism, there are likewise compelling reasons for both sides to seek fruitful security cooperation, and Afghanistan is a good place to start.

The American Rationale.

The fanatics responsible for September 11, 2001 (9/11), must be brought to justice, and their successors must be denied bases from which U.S. and allied targets can be struck. Osama bin Laden's death is a start, but there is a lot more work to be done to deter further jihadist attacks. The Taliban continues to harbor al-Qaeda, and a Kabul government under its control would be intolerable. If the American-led campaign to destroy al-Qaeda and neutralize the Taliban in Afghanistan fails, U.S. and allied security will be placed at grave risk:

- The United States may once again be struck by jihadists operating from a Taliban-controlled

3

Afghanistan, only this time with weapons of mass destruction (WMD).

- Emboldened, the jihadists will try to topple moderate and pro-American governments throughout the Greater Middle East including Egypt, Israel, Jordan, and Saudi Arabia.
- A jihadist victory in Afghanistan will encourage their counterparts in Pakistan to overthrow the government or foment upheaval that ignites a nuclear showdown with India.
- A campaign to create an Islamic Caliphate is far-fetched, but the chaos and violence that it will spawn will disrupt the production and flow of hydrocarbons to the world market.
- Central Asia, which is strategically linked to Afghanistan and is a region vital to the world's energy market, is vulnerable to jihadist movements. They will be emboldened to subvert the region should the West's venture in Afghanistan fail.

The Russian Rationale.

Russian strategists cite a number of reasons why a Taliban victory in Afghanistan will place Russia's security at risk:

- About 90 percent of the heroin that is consumed by drug addicts in Russia comes from Afghanistan's fields and laboratories. It is no surprise, then, that the Russian public deems drug abuse to be their society's gravest social problem and the major rationale for cooperating with the West in Afghanistan.
- If the jihadists are successful in Afghanistan, they will mount a campaign to topple pro-Rus-

sian governments throughout Central Asia and deny Moscow strategic space.

- Jihadists who have been supporting the North Caucasus insurgents will be emboldened and provide arms and fighters to further inflame violent insurrection in the region and deeper into Russia proper.
- Under these circumstances, Putin and Medvedev's campaign to restore Russia's power through a modernization drive will be placed in peril.

The Study's Objectives.

It is the purpose of this paper to address a series of questions that consider the existing status of U.S.-Russian cooperation and the prospects for future joint security ventures in the region. A second major objective will be to take stock of U.S. accomplishments and failures to date as it prepares for the 2014 exit from Afghanistan. It will set in motion a host of reactions from stakeholders who have been functioning as bystanders but henceforth will become more actively engaged in finding a resolution to the conflict. Pertinent questions that need to be asked include the following:

- How did the Soviet invasion of Afghanistan and the U.S.-led response to it conspire to create both al-Qaeda and the Taliban?
- Could a civil war have been avoided had the Cold War superpowers collaborated and replaced a communist government in Kabul with one that represented a broad cross-section of Afghan society?
- How has Russia assisted the American-led International Security Assistance Force (ISAF)

mission in its campaign to destroy al-Qaeda and to dismantle the Taliban, thereby denying the jihadists a return to power in Kabul?

- What are the prospects that the U.S. counterinsurgency (COIN) strategy will succeed and, if it fails, what are the alternatives?
- How might Moscow assist Washington under a medley of possible outcomes as the starting point for the transition to Afghan security forces approaches? To properly address this question, we must explore Russia's activities in Afghanistan over the past several decades.
- Who are the other major players in the Afghanistan Question, and have we properly identified the enemy? In this last connection, what has been labeled "global terrorism" may be understood more appropriately as a civil war within the Islamic community. If so, what changes should be made in our response to it?
- What impact will the U.S. public opposition to the war in Afghanistan—and mounting concerns about America's economic plight—have upon a COIN strategy that rests on two major variables: time and, in essence, nation-building?
- Why has the time come to negotiate with the Taliban, and what are the prospects of a successful outcome? Why do reconciliation with the Taliban and the stabilization of Afghanistan necessitate a broad diplomatic approach to the Afghanistan Question?
- With the approach of the U.S. 2012 presidential elections, why must the United States reassess its relations with Pakistan? How can both sides work toward a successful outcome in Afghanistan in spite of their strained relations?

- Against the backdrop of a changing international strategic environment and malaise at home, has the time come for the United States to reduce its military profile in the Greater Middle East?
- Why can it be argued that the U.S. military has accomplished its mission in Afghanistan but henceforth must address the jihadist threat through counterterrorism (CT) and not COIN operations?
- Finally, readers of this paper should recall the words of Secretary Gates in his last policy speech as U.S. Defense Secretary in Brussels, Belgium, on June 10, 2011: ". . . true friends occasionally must speak bluntly with one another for the sake of those greater interests and values that bind us together."

CHAPTER 1

THE SOVIET INVASION OF AFGHANISTAN

THE DECISION TO INVADE

On December 12, 1979, three old men in the Politburo gave a green light to invade Afghanistan. The troika included the foreign minister, Andrei Gromyko; the Committee for State Security (KGB) director, Yuri Andropov; and the minister of defense, Dmitri Ustinov. They would serve on the Politburo's Afghanistan Commission and encourage the aging General Secretary of the Central Committee of the Communist Party of the Soviet Union (CPSU), Leonid Brezhnev, to endorse the first use of the Red Army outside of the Soviet empire since World War II. They were responding to the Kabul government's request to save the communist revolution in Afghanistan.

In the process, the Soviet overlords ignored those in the military high command who deemed the operation ill-advised. In their assessment, Afghanistan was of no strategic value, and for centuries the primitive people living there had demonstrated that they were resolute fighters who skillfully exploited their homeland's rough terrain to defeat invaders, even those with superior arms and resources.[1] Some Western analysts saw the invasion as a Soviet drive toward the Indian Ocean in keeping with the Czars' dream of a warm water port, but the truth was that the Kremlin oligarchs discounted the high command's advice in order to save a pro-Soviet government in Kabul and to prevent the United States from securing a foothold in the region. After their expulsion from Iran, the Americans were looking for bases in Central Asia to encircle the Union of Soviet Socialist Republics (USSR). From Afghanistan, they could destabilize the Central Asia Republics and, in turn, place the Soviet regime at risk. Some in the Kremlin feared the United States would deploy missiles that were programmed to hit targets in the Soviet Union.[2]

The Afghan drama began in April 1978 in what became known as the Saur (April) Revolution when pro-Soviet elements gained power upon the assassination of President Mohammed Daoud. He had assumed political authority in a July 1973 military coup amid charges of corruption and misrule associated with his cousin Zahir Shah. The latter's downfall would spell the end of the Afghanistan monarchy and spawn decades of warfare in one of the world's most remote and backward countries. Ironically, the Soviet-trained commandos who killed Daoud were from the same unit that had helped him achieve power 5 years earlier. He had angered Moscow when he loosened his ties with the Kremlin and removed communists from his cabinet. He made a huge blunder when he arrested the communist leader Nur Mohammed Taraki, but only placed his associate, Hafizullah Amin, under house arrest. With the help of friendly members of the military, Amin launched a coup that resulted in Daoud's murder.

Taraki was an intellectual like most members of the Marxist People's Democratic Party of Afghanistan (PDPA), and this would inform his conduct as prime minister. He openly expressed admiration for Lenin's brutal suppression of his enemies and, once in power, would follow a similar course. He belonged to the Khalq (Masses) faction of the party which competed for power with a second communist faction, the Parcham (Banner), controlled by Babrak Karmal.

Ideological and ethnic differences divided the two organizations, and these fissures would prove to be destabilizing. Khalq was largely comprised of "Pashtun" and Parcham "non-Pashtun" members.

Once in control, Taraki subverted Islamic influence in the country and imposed strict Marxist rule upon it. Initially, his benefactors in Moscow failed to appreciate that in his open hostility toward Islam, Taraki was engaging in a disastrous enterprise. They suffered from the same myopia about religion that afflicted the Shah of Iran's Washington supporters. The mullahs of Iran toppled him earlier in the year. Indeed, there were advisers who counseled President Carter to launch a military campaign to oust the Islamic rulers—an option that we know now would have been disastrous and almost certain to fail.[3]

The Soviets "failed initially to detect the virus of Islamist militancy spreading north and east from Tehran through informal and underground networks."[4] Moscow's Middle East allies were ruled by secular regimes like those in Syria, Iraq, and Central Asia, so the Russians did not fully appreciate the power of religion in backward Afghanistan. "Like the Americans, the Soviets had directed most of their resources and talent toward the ideological battlefields of Europe and Asia during the previous 2 decades."[5]

ESCALATION

After a traumatic March 1979 uprising in Herat, Taraki pleaded with Moscow for Soviet troops to save the Marxist government in Kabul. The Iranians had spread their Islamic revolution to the Farsi-speaking Afghan city because the Shiite residents were emboldened by the success of the Islamic Shiite revolutionaries living across their western border. Devout leaders in Herat were outraged when the pro-Soviet government embarked upon an education program for girls, usurped tribal lands, and waged a war on Islamic religious practices. Encouraged by their Iranian neighbors, Islamic radicals in Herat took up arms against the Soviet advisors, and many Russians, including women and children, were slaughtered in the uprising.

After the Herat atrocities, the Soviets provided the Afghan army with more weapons and additional military advisers to assist them in meeting mounting resistance. If there were any doubts in Moscow about growing instability, they vanished when an entire Afghan division later mutinied and the troops moved on Kabul. They were crushed, but Soviet military commanders, who anticipated an early exit from Afghanistan with the creation of a loyal local army, had to accept a disconcerting truth: the Red Army was headed for a fight with the resolute mujahedeen and would remain in Afghanistan for many years. Meanwhile, some members of the Soviet political elite feared that, in his march toward a Soviet Afghanistan, Afghan communist party boss Taraki was moving too quickly. They were in a minority, but events would prove them right.

The Herat uprising lost Taraki friends in Moscow, and, worse yet, it poisoned relations with his Afghan comrades. The split among the communists resulted in his September assassination. He was replaced by Hafizullah Amin who at one time attended Columbia University but left disgruntled when he was denied his degree. He would not be around for long either. His fate was sealed, in part, as a result of a KGB "blowback" operation whereby he was accused of being a Central Intelligence Agency (CIA) agent. Soviet intelligence at one time had made that charge possibly because of his American education. Also, after Amin's fall meeting with U.S. diplomats in Kabul, some in the Kremlin feared that their man was moving toward an alliance with the Americans and their "Pakistani puppets."

Out of desperation, Moscow replaced him with Babrak Karmal and settled the crisis in Afghanistan by invading the country. Some in the Kremlin were aiming less to save a Marxist brother than to create a firewall between the aroused Muslim fanatics to their south, and Soviet citizens of the Islamic faith. The most obvious targets were the five Soviet Central Asian Republics (the "Stans") where most of the inhabitants were Muslims. For these pragmatic strategists, the issue of internal Soviet security transcended that of international solidarity. Karmal was a gifted speaker but would prove to be a weak leader, and he spent much of his time savaging his opponents in the PDPA. For him, the playing field was Kabul and Afghanistan's larger cities; like his comrades, he avoided the countryside where the party had little influence and its Marxist policies fostered much hostility.

The Kremlin leaders did not think the Red Army would be in Afghanistan for long and this was the consensus of the international community. Many in the West believed that the Soviet planners reached this conclusion as a result of their quick suppression of the Czech Spring in 1968. However, later Russian commenters have rejected that facile notion and provided another one instead. Namely, the mujahedeen were poorly armed, illiterate peasants without modern means of transport or communications. How could they possibility resist World War II's most powerful fighting force and one of the Cold War's premier military powers?

Throughout the conflict, the Soviets and their Afghan allies controlled the major towns while the countryside was dominated by the mujahedeen. The communists enjoyed a huge advantage in fire power; in addition to tanks and artillery, they dominated the air with helicopters, bombers, and fighter aircraft. They also had modern communication equipment that gave them an edge in battle. Although logistics were difficult, their grunts did not have to worry about counting their ammunition as the enemy did.

Their strategy was a simple one; deny the insurgent's access to the people by brutally punishing ordinary folk. The Red Army went about its bloody business with artillery, airstrikes, and massive armor attacks. To deny the mujahedeen access to roads and other transportation nodes, they laid millions of mines, often by air. As a consequence, more than one million Afghans died in the war, and millions more would flee the country to Iran and Pakistan. Many of the three million that sought refuge in Pakistan would be transformed into dedicated Islamic warriors after occupying refugee camps and attending madrassas operated by radical Islamists. Here they would combine their nationalistic sensibilities with a new messianic religious impulse and embrace a narrative that the Arab Islamists were crafting for them and Muslims throughout the world — Global Jihad.

During the course of the war, 620,000 Soviet soldiers served in Afghanistan. At their peak, there were 120,000 Soviet troops in country, and officially they suffered almost 15,000 deaths, while 60,000 were injured and hospitalized for physical and psychological reasons.[6] In contrast to the insurgents, the Soviet casualties were modest. Nonetheless, the Red Army did not have the appropriate doctrine to crush its enemies, and its reliance upon heavy tanks and large columns of infantry proved to be disastrous. As their casualties mounted and their sacrifices produced paltry results, the morale of Soviet soldiers took a nosedive. It did not help that they often did not have faith in their officers who brutally mistreated them. In response, the soldiers sought solace in alcohol and drugs. When they did not have the money to purchase these diversions, they sold their weapons and ammunition. Soviet commanders were tormented by this behavior and appalled by reports that many troops from Central Asia were finding common cause with their ethnic brethren. Military planners had assumed that in the initial stages of the invasion, it made sense to deploy soldiers who shared common cultural, lingual, and religious bonds with the Afghans. To their dismay, however, they got reports that these troops sympathized with the rebels and, in some cases, joined them on the battlefield or travelled to Pakistan where they were introduced to radical jihadist ideas. Consequently,

> less than 4 months after the beginning of the conflict, in March 1980, Moscow had to recall a large part of the Central Asian reservists deployed in Kabul. At the same time there were anti-war demonstrations in Tajik, Turkmen and Uzbek communities within the USSR. Defense analysts were especially alarmed by reports of mujahedeen military forays into Soviet territory where these people lived.[7]

Of course, things turned decidedly worse for the Soviet soldiers when the mujahedeen received modern arms, artillery, heavy machine guns, rockets, and anti-aircraft systems from the Americans, Chinese, Iranians, Pakistanis, and Saudis. They also were joined by fanatical and tough Islamic warriors from the Middle

East, Southeast Asia, and even Russia itself. The "for-eigners," however, never provided the number of fighters that the "locals" did.

Simultaneously, while some of the Soviet's Afghan allies fought effectively, others did not. Many of them left their units and returned home or even joined the mujahedeen when the going got rough. Throughout their history, fighters in Afghanistan often changed sides for a variety of reasons and did much the same thing during the Soviet war.

Although outgunned, the rebels were familiar with the difficult terrain, and large numbers of them shared a common language and culture. Even if they belonged to disparate ethnic communities, they all resented Soviet troops in their country. The common bond of religion was one of their most powerful as-sets, and they were often protected by their neigh-bors who forewarned them when a larger advancing Soviet force threatened their units. The mujahedeen had been reared in a martial culture, and most knew how to use firearms; besides that, they were brave and motivated by a deep hatred of their occupiers. They had endured hardships that their Soviet counterparts had not encountered in private life, and they did not need the massive supplies that helped sustain the en-emy. Unlike the Soviet soldiers, they were fighting for their country and Allah, and were prepared to out-wait their enemies. When faced with a superior force, they vanished from the battlefield and only returned to ambush surprised opponents. In sum, following the dictates of Mao, they fought only when they had an advantage and avoided contact with their enemy when it was comprised of a larger fighting force.

After a period of failed operations, the Soviet military adopted new tactics that relied primarily upon rapid strikes by jets and helicopters, along with small-unit operations spearheaded by bold airborne ambushes. They sought to seal off the border with Pakistan, and on occasion Soviet planes overflew its territory. The Soviet leaders, however, never contemplated major incursions in Pakistan — the only effective way to halt the flow of fighters and their equipment into Afghanistan. The sanctuaries and the ability of the mujahedeen to duck into elaborate tunnel networks or vanish in rugged mountain terrain denied the Red Army the set-piece battles at which they excelled.

> Among the more successful Soviet operations in late 1981 was a series of offensives in Nangrahar Province near the Pakistan border and a winter offensive in Parwan, where Soviet and Afghan forces crushed much of the resistance activity in the province. Recounting these successes, Mark Urban, a perceptive British historian of war, observed that "they gave the Soviet army a new operational confidence." It was this upbeat mood, Urban said, that led to more aggressive tactics during 1982, symbolized, in particular, by the climactic Panjshir offensives of May and August — the biggest battles of the entire war.[8]

The Panjshir Valley was territory controlled by the Tajik commander Ahmed Shah Massoud, but while the Soviets could clear territory, they could never hold it. That drove the generals to distraction, but their civilian masters in Moscow had calculated that more troops meant more casualties, and that clearly was out of the question. The Kremlin leaders did not have to pay the same heed to public opinion that their democratic counterparts did, but they could not ignore it altogether.

Over the next several years, the enemy continued to suffer heavy casualties, but in the spring of 1985, Soviet planners faced two powerful barriers to victory. First, after Mikhail Gorbachev became General Secretary of the CPSU, he concluded that the war was a lost cause, speaking of it as a "bleeding wound." Things were getting so bad that Soviet authorities, in a campaign to assuage public opposition, minimized the casualties that the Army endured. Second, there was reason to believe that the war could be won but only with a massive infusion of Soviet troops; one American analyst spoke in terms of 500,000. It was not altogether clear whether Moscow had the logistical capability to provide for a larger force, even if it was available. Simultaneously, the Kremlin was not prepared to accept the certain subsequent rise in casualties.

BRINGING THE RED ARMY HOME

In a November 1986 meeting of the Politburo, Gorbachev told his comrades, "The strategic goal is to finish the war in 1, maximum 2, years and withdraw the troops. We have set a clear goal: Help speed up the process so we have a friendly neutral country, and get out of there."[9] He assumed that he could convince the Americans that it was in their interest to establish a moderate regime in Kabul — but he would have little success in making his case with them. They smelled blood and were in no mood to allow the Soviets to find a painless exit from Afghanistan.

From the very outset of the Afghan war, all of the Soviet leaders, including some hardliners who wholeheartedly supported it, worried about the war harming relations with Washington. They felt obligated to help their comrades in the Third World but not at the expense of détente with the United States, the only country with the capacity to defeat the USSR in a nuclear exchange.

Still, Gorbachev was slow in bringing the Red Army home because he believed that Moscow's National Reconciliation Program might stabilize Afghanistan and, in the final analysis, keep a pro-Soviet government in Kabul. In a word, it was nothing less than a nation-building campaign that rested on improving the lives of the Afghans so that they would turn away from the jihadists and embrace the communist government instead. Simultaneously, Gorbachev lectured the Afghan elite upon the imperatives of reaching out to the peasants, and even to political opponents, and not being too harsh on Islam. As a consequence of his dalliance, more people died on all sides. Indeed, like his predecessors, Gorbachev delayed the pullout for the simple reason that while the status quo was hardly encouraging, the USSR was not suffering too much on the diplomatic front and the costs in lives and treasure were acceptable. Jimmy Carter imposed a grain embargo upon the USSR, but Canada and Australia did not honor it, and Moscow could live with the casualties, given the huge size of the Red Army along with war-related expenses. For example, over a 4-year period in the late 1980s, the war cost $7.5 billion, but the Soviet defense budget in 1989 was $128 billion.[10]

A Soviet military solution to the Afghan insurgency became even more unlikely as the supply of new fighters from Pakistan entered the country. The Arabs among them who were bankrolled by Saudi Arabia, and Osama bin Laden himself, were dedicated warriors although their numbers were small. In addition, sophisticated arms from friendly supporters had helped reduce the hardware advantage that the Red Army had earlier enjoyed. For example, Stinger anti-aircraft missiles forced the Soviets to reconfigure their helicopter and fixed-wing aircraft operations and clearly emboldened the mujahedeen while demoralizing their enemies. Perhaps the Stingers' impact upon the war have been exaggerated, but they, and other arms provided the Afghan fighters, encouraged the enemy to leave their country.[11]

That said, after changing tactics the Soviet military's performance in Afghanistan improved dramatically, prompting Mark Katz to observe: "Had it not been for the weapons, training, and other support provided to the guerrillas by the United States, Saudi Arabia, China, and Pakistan, Soviet troops undoubtedly would have been able to crush the resistance and achieve an outright victory."[12]

That conclusion reflected unwarranted confidence in the ability of outside conventional forces to defeat a resolute army of indigenous insurgents who have the option of fighting when they choose to; warriors, one might add, that in contrast to the enemy relied upon a smaller amount of equipment and food and medicine to sustain themselves. What is more, insurgents have an enormous advantage when facing foreign troops who simply do not understand the strong cultural factors that thrive in any social system. As a consequence, locals do not need intelligence briefings to separate their neighbors from the foreign invaders. Then, too, ordinary Afghans had more in common with the jihadists — even if strangers — than they did with "alien infidels."

In the final analysis, when in trouble the weary Russian invaders resorted to the application of brute force with little regard for civilian casualties that characterized their operations in other places, like Grozny years later. In measuring the Red Army's failure to defeat the insurgents by brutalizing the civilian population, one analyst underscores the method's pitfalls:

- It could not "overcome the mujahedeen determination to resist the Soviet occupation based on the insurgents' religious and nationalistic beliefs."
- "Instead of pacifying the population, these actions incited even greater resistance."
- The Soviets could not compel people to support a regime viewed as illegitimate by the majority of the Afghan population.

At the same time, when commenting on why the Soviets failed to impose military defeat upon the mujahedeen, the analyst makes the following observations:

- The insurgents enjoyed the protection of sanctuaries.
- Their minimal logistical requirements were an asset.
- The Soviets did not have sufficient troops, especially those with counterinsurgency training, to defeat the mujahedeen.
- The Soviets lacked appropriate counterinsurgency doctrine.
- The introduction of effective man-portable surface-to-air missile (SAM) technology dramatically negated Soviet air supremacy.[13]

In short, these lessons underscore the natural advantages enjoyed by local insurgents who are protecting their turf and are prepared to endure unimaginable costs for the simple reason that they have nowhere else to go. At the same time, the Afghans had been fighting for decades, were skilled in small-unit operations, and, fortified by their religious convictions, ignored overwhelming odds against victory. As a consequence of fighting alongside more sophisticated Arab comrades, many of these simple folk became infused with a new brand of religious zeal, one that presented them with the prospect of joining the international jihadi movement.

For the Arab jihadists, the Afghan battlefield was preparing them for a showdown with the corrupt and faithless leaders that ruled over them back home and eventually with the Americans who stood in the way of the Caliphate that many of them dreamed about. It puzzled Western analysts that in scanning the bios of many of these young fighters, it was discovered that they were often better educated than their brethren back home and did not necessarily come from the ranks of the economically and socially deprived. In other words, they represented a force for modernization, not reaction.

WHAT WAS HAPPENING?

One possible key to this puzzle was revealed decades ago when Western political scientists first began studying the newly independent nations of Africa, Asia, and Latin America — the less developed countries (LDCs) — and made a surprising discovery. Those migrants who were leaving the traditional countryside for the city — that is, the most "modern" elements of their communities — rediscovered their ethnic, religious, and tribal roots in the harsh crucible of urban life. In short, they found a safe harbor in traditional associations, identities, and values that they had scorned back in the village.[14] This link between the old and new has become a toxic brew in many areas of the Islamic world and is the basis for revolutionary upheaval throughout it.

THE U.S. REACTION

The American intelligence community failed to anticipate the Soviet invasion in what was seen as a backwater region in a remote part of the world and of scant strategic value. Various intelligence agencies detected the Soviet military buildup north of Afghanistan before the invasion, but there was no consensus as to its significance.

In mid-December 1978, additional Soviet units joined the small number of units already in Afghanistan. This revelation compelled U.S. intelligence to conclude that an invasion was in the works, but its magnitude and longevity remained uncertain. After the Soviets expelled Amin, it was clear that a full-fledged invasion was about to begin.

Meanwhile, President Carter indicated that he would welcome harmonious relations with Moscow, following the road to détente blazed by the Richard Nixon administration. But if the Kremlin expected him to accept the invasion without a response, it was sadly mistaken. Carter proclaimed that "the Soviet invasion of Afghanistan is the greatest threat to peace since the Second World War. It's a sharp escalation in the aggressive history of the Soviet Union."[15] He cancelled grain exports to the USSR, blocked the sale of hi-tech items, boycotted the 1980 Olympics, and pulled the Strategic Arms Limitation Talks (SALT) II Treaty from Senate consideration.

In February 1979, relations between Washington and Kabul plunged further when the U.S. Ambassador, Adolph Dubs, was kidnapped by radicals and later killed when Afghan government troops tried to free him. Several months later, upon the advice of his national security advisor, Zbigniew Brzezinski, Carter ordered the CIA to provide the mujahedeen with a modest supply of arms, finances, and training. When Ronald Reagan succeeded Carter, the United States continued that practice and raised the costs that the Soviets were enduring in a fight that was being characterized as "their Vietnam." "By 1984, CIA funding was approaching $350 million annually and peaked in 1987 and 1988 at close to $400 million."[16] At the same time, Washington provided Pakistan with a huge civilian and military aid package resulting in its becoming the third leading recipient of U.S. largess. Here, we see an American administration setting aside its values in favor of its interests. Not only was Pakistan a dictatorship, it was striving, in opposition to U.S. policy, to become a nuclear power. That effort had prompted the passage of the Pressler amendment that conditioned U.S. economic aid to Pakistan on its willingness to give up its quest for nukes. With the Red Army in Afghanistan, relations between the United States and Pakistan moved in a harmonious direction.

It was through the Pakistani Inter-Services Intelligence Directorate (ISI) that U.S. aid was delivered, and the Pakistani security services in the process secured close ties with the mujahedeen. Meanwhile, Pakistani General Muhammad ul-Haq Zia was alarmed by the Iran revolution, and when the Red Army entered Afghanistan, he feared his country might be next. All of his associates expressed concern about the Soviet-Indian connection and feared that a pro-Indian government in Afghanistan represented a serious threat to Pakistan.

The Pakistanis therefore were happy to provide the anti-Soviet fighters with a safe haven that enabled them to rest, train, and recruit for a surging resistance movement in Afghanistan. One might observe that as long as that circumstance obtained, a Soviet military victory was implausible. With the help of Pakistan's ISI, the CIA coordinated the delivery of arms, food, equipment, and medicine to the mujahedeen. The ISI played much the same role in delivering Saudi Arabia's money to the mujahedeen. In the process, it not only developed close relations with the fighters, it became apparent that, should they be victorious, Pakistan could use them to advance its own interests in a post-Soviet Afghanistan and help wrest control of Kashmir from India—one of the few major countries not to condemn the Soviet invasion. Toward this end, it supported Hafez Saeed who, along with Abdallah Azzam, had founded Lashkar-e-Tayyiba, the jihadist organization that was committed to that goal.

At the same time, fundamentalist mullahs inculcated young Afghan men with the most radical interpretation of the Koran and mesmerized them with the prospect of an Islamic movement that someday would create a Caliphate uniting Muslims worldwide. This noble ideal would be fed by hatred of indigenous infidels and the Westerners who had subjugated the faithful for centuries.

The conflicting strategic perspectives of Washington and Islamabad were ignored by American officials as they focused on the immediate objective of expelling the Soviets from Afghanistan. Preoccupied with the short term, U.S. analysts did not ask a fundamental question: "Whose side would the mujahedeen be on after the Soviets left the country?" What is more, it must have been unnerving for those Americans who had followed developments there to acknowledge that there was a direct correlation between the most effective fighters and hostility toward the infidels, domestic and foreign. U.S. officials then had reason to anticipate the Soviet Union's exit from Afghanistan with some trepidation. But they were taking such satisfaction in the USSR's obvious foreign policy disaster that they did not give much thought to what would happen next.

On December 4, 1987, Robert Gates, then acting CIA director, broke bread at a Washington restaurant with Vladimir Kryuchkov, his KGB counterpart. The latter observed that the Soviets were preparing to leave Afghanistan, but they would need U.S. help in finding a political solution to the conflict. This had been the message of his boss who was saying the same thing to Reagan. Among other things, Gorbachev wanted Washington to halt aiding the Afghan rebels when the Soviets withdrew. Indeed, this was Moscow's bottom line but in a subsequent meeting with Reagan, Gorbachev was informed that the United States could not honor his request. Reagan and his advisers knew that Gorbachev was desperate to get out, and the Americans held the high hand.

In his meeting with Gates, Vladimir Kryuchkov indicated that the Kremlin feared radical Islamists might gain power in Kabul. Then he noted, "You seem fully occupied in trying to deal with just one fundamentalist Islamic state,"[17] meaning that there was a host of "bad guys" who were prepared to destabilize Afghanistan after the Soviets left, in the hope of securing control of Kabul. There was substance to this observation, for while the Reagan administration was clear about wanting the Soviets out, it had no well-defined policy regarding the new government other than that the radical jihadists had to be denied power. All available evidence, however, indicated that without outside intervention, facts on the ground dictated a radical Islamist victory in Afghanistan.

THE END

On February 8, 1988, the world was shocked to learn that Gorbachev had decided to withdraw Soviet forces from Afghanistan. The formal terms of a Soviet withdrawal were ratified on April 14 at Geneva, Switzerland. In addition to the Afghan communist government, the document was signed by Pakistan, the Soviet Union, and the United States. The rebels were excluded from the negotiations, but Washington would continue to supply them with military material.

Reagan, in response to Gorbachev's assertion that the United States had to halt arms transfers to the mujahedeen, answered that that would be impossible as long as the Kremlin continued to render similar support to Najibullah, the former head of the Afghan State Information Service or secret police. Najibullah had been chosen to replace Karmal because, unlike the latter, he was competent and strong physically and mentally. Consequently, Gorbachev believed he could survive a Soviet exit from Afghanistan—at least long enough to find a settlement that did not humiliate the USSR. In hoping to achieve this goal, he looked expectantly toward Washington.

Those in Moscow who believed the Kremlin could develop harmonious relations with Washington were heartened by the 1987 Intermediate-Range Nuclear Force (INF) Treaty outlawing intermediate-range ballistic missiles. After all, that deal was made possible by Reagan, the man who many Soviet hardliners reviled since he was the captive of "unrepentant Cold Warriors" in the United States. The former movie actor, who would help develop a narrative for America's future that even the Democrats would have to accept, had come to the conclusion that it was in the nation's vital interest to cooperate with the USSR in making the world a safer place through arms control. In so doing, he shocked many of his admirers who believed in absolute security through nuclear dominance and rejected joint ventures of any kind with the Soviets.

Many of the people around Gorbachev, like his Foreign Minister Eduard Shevardnadze, bitterly opposed a deal that compromised Najibullah's prospects for surviving a Soviet withdrawal and deemed the Geneva Agreement as tilted against him. Gorbachev ignored the advice because a diplomatic settlement was in keeping with his New Thinking on domestic and international affairs. In his mind, they were interconnected since liberal policies at home and a new positive relationship with the United States abroad would set the Soviet Union on a new track—one that would lead it out of the morass that his predecessors had bequeathed to him.

On February 15 the following year, the commander of the 40th Army, General Boris Gromov, led his troops over the Termez Bridge to Uzbekistan, and the Soviet invasion and occupation of Afghanistan were history. In the eyes of the world, the Red Army had suffered a massive defeat, even though there was justification for Gromov's claim that no "Soviet garrison or major outpost" had ever been overrun by the enemy. In every set-piece battle with the Soviets, their enemy lost.[18] But no matter how sugar-coatedly the military high command sought to characterize their exit from

Afghanistan, the Red Army's reputation suffered a huge setback. For disgruntled and restive people in the "Outer Soviet Empire"—the satellites in Eastern Europe—and the "Inner-Empire"—the non-Russian Republics—the luster of the mighty Red Army was profoundly tarnished. Unquestionably, the setback in Afghanistan emboldened opponents of the Soviet regime throughout the empire and contributed to its eventual demise in December 1991. But,

> while many expected the departure of the Soviet army in February 1989 to mark the end of the war, it did not. The Najibullah regime—aided by Soviet security assistance—was clever and built alliances around the country. With a 65,000-man army, an air force of nearly 200 planes and helicopters, and many well-paid militia units, Afghan government forces were able to hold off the mujahideen. This fact became clear in May 1989, when a number of mujahideen groups attacked, but failed to seize, the city of Jalalabad in eastern Afghanistan.[19]

ENDNOTES - CHAPTER 1

1. For an American depiction of the war, see Gregory Feifer, *The Great Gamble: The Soviet War in Afghanistan*, New York: Harper Perennial, 2009, p. 11. A Soviet perspective is provided by Artyom Borovik, *The Hidden War*, New York: Atlantic Monthly Press, 1990.

2. Feifer, p. 3. Artemy M. Kalinovsky explains why, in spite of fears in the Kremlin about American strategic interests in the area, the Soviet leaders were reluctant to invade Afghanistan. See his *A Long Goodbye*, Boston, MA: Harvard University Press, 2011. This book relies upon Russian material that heretofore has not been released.

3. In this connection, see Patrick Tyler, *A World of Trouble*, New York: Farrar Straus and Giroux, 2009, p. 233.

4. Diego Cordovez and Selig S. Harrison, *Out of Afghanistan*, New York: Oxford University Press, 1995.

5. *Ibid.*

6. Marlene Laruelle, *Beyond the Afghan Trauma: Russia's Return to Afghanistan*, Washington, DC: The Jamestown Foundation, August 2009, p. 22.

7. *Ibid.* Also, as a consequence of serving in Afghanistan, thousands of Central Asians were introduced to radical versions of Islam and, upon returning home, became proponents of religious notions that did not sit well with the Kremlin. See Ahmed Rashid, *Jihad: The Rise of Militant Islam in Central Asia*, New Haven, CT: Yale University Press, 2002.

8. Cordovez and Harrison, p. 71.

9. Steve Coll, *Ghost Wars*, New York: Penguin Books, 2004, p. 158.

10. Kalinovsky, p. 42.

11. *Ibid.*, p. 43.

12. Mark Katz, "The Soviet Military Experience in Afghanistan: A Precedent of Dubious Relevance," PONARS Policy Memo 202, October 2001, p. 1.

13. Edward B. Westermann, "The Limits of Soviet Airpower: The Failure of Military Coercion in Afghanistan, 1979-89," Thesis, Air University, Maxwell Air Force Base, Montgomery, AL, 1997, pp. 15-16.

14. I observed this when I wrote a doctoral dissertation for Georgetown University that assessed the relationship between urbanization and political development in the Third World.

15. Robert M. Gates, *From The Shadows: The Ultimate Insider's Story of Five Presidents and How They Won the Cold War*, New York: Simon & Schuster, 1996, p. 425.

16. Major James T. McGhee, "The Soviet Experience in Afghanistan: Lessons Learned," *MilitaryHistoryOnline.com*, June 14, 2008, p. 1.

17. Bruce Riedel, *Deadly Embrace*, Washington, DC: Brookings Institution Press, 2011, p. 27.

18. Steve Galster, "Volume II: Lessons from the Last War," The National Security Archive, October 9, 2001, p. 25. For a comprehensive treatment of the diplomacy leading up to the Soviet exit from Afghanistan, see Cordovez and Harrison.

19. Joseph J. Collins, *Understanding War in Afghanistan*, Washington, DC: National Defense University Press, 2010, p. 35.

CHAPTER 2

THE FAILURE TO CREATE
A STABLE POST-SOVIET GOVERNMENT
AND CIVIL WAR

THE UNITED NATIONS PROPOSAL

The Soviet invasion of Afghanistan had been roundly condemned internationally, so Gorbachev's diplomatic leverage was minimal. In particular, his effort to sustain the Najibullah regime in Kabul was a hard sell. His reputation as a brutal torturer hardly burnished his image before the international community.

On January 14, 1980, the United Nations (UN) by a margin of 144 to 18, with 18 abstentions, called for the withdrawal of "foreign troops" from Afghanistan. Years later, under the direction of Diego Cordovez, the Ecuadorian diplomat, the UN explored a path to a cease-fire that was acceptable to all parties to the dispute. The proposal that he crafted rested on three major propositions:

1. Najibullah's regime was unacceptable to most Afghans and had to be replaced by a provisional government.

2. It would be broad-based and include communists, the resistance fighters, and the émigrés that over the decades of fighting had fled the country. A pivotal figure in this connection was the former elderly King who Cordovez believed was the only person who was acceptable to both sides.

3. Progress would not occur as long as both the Soviet Union and the United States continued to provide the combatants with arms.[1]

On September 13, 1991, U.S. Secretary of State James Baker and his Soviet counterpart Boris Pankin agreed to cut off aid to their Afghan clients. It was at this point that the fate of Najibullah was sealed. As he contemplated his imminent demise, he told reporters, "If fundamentalism comes to Afghanistan, war will continue for many years. Afghanistan will turn into a center of world smuggling for narcotic drugs. Afghanistan will be turned into a center for terrorism."[2] At the behest of the UN representative in Kabul, he agreed to forfeit power in favor of a government formed under the international body.

Najibullah survived the Soviet withdrawal for several years, in no small part because he skillfully arranged deals with disparate warlords. But in September 1991 just weeks after the anti-Gorbachev coup, the UN campaign to arrange a peaceful settlement between Najibullah and his opponents collapsed. Najibullah's fortunes took a further turn for the worse when his Uzbek ally, Aburrashid Dostum, joined one of the most gifted anti-Soviet leaders, Ahmed Shah Massoud, and provided the Tajik with an additional fighting force of 40,000 men, along with tanks, artillery, and aircraft. A third major mujahedeen commander, Gulbuddin Hekmatyar, joined them as well. A Pashtun, he was a favorite of the Pakistani Directorate for Inter-Services Intelligence (ISI) and would become a close associate of Osama bin Laden, with whom he shared profound anti-American sentiments. This troika of warlords would overwhelm Najibullah's demoralized units and, in the face of certain defeat, he sought refuge in the UN compound where he lived until he was killed by the Taliban. His life would have been spared had he accepted Massoud's advice to leave Kabul before the Taliban attacked the city.

WHY THE PROPOSAL FAILED

In the final analysis, UN-inspired efforts to accomplish a peaceful transition of power in Afghanistan failed. There were simply too many hurdles. As the transition of security to Karzai's forces commences today, U.S. analysts searching for a solution to the present conflict in Afghanistan would be well-advised to consider all of those hurdles.

- The Kremlin persisted in the claim that Najibullah's government could serve as an interim authority, but that proposal was a non-starter for all the other players in the drama. Not only was his regime deemed illegitimate by most Afghans, it was riven by conflict. It also was incapable of functioning effectively without extensive outside help, and that dependency hobbled the Afghan communists in their campaign to survive the Soviets' exit from the country. "The presence of Soviet troops and advisers seemed to cause paralysis among Afghan politicians. This may have been due to a sense that the Soviet advisers could do the job better, or it may have been a response to the generally imperial attitude adopted by some advisers."[3]
- The resistance leaders in Afghanistan—known as the "Peshawar Seven," a group of powerful opponents that included the country's future president, Burhanuddin Rabbani—were at odds with one another. Moreover, one of the most dominant commanders in opposition to the UN proposal was Hekmatyar. He complained, "Cordovez has always been trying to prove that the Afghan crisis is indigenous

while we have been fighting against foreign aggression. As soon as the foreign intervention ends, peace will be restored in Afghanistan."[4]

- Pakistan would not accept a provisional government that it considered to be unfavorable to its strategic concerns, and it could count upon the support of Saudi Arabia to follow its lead on these matters. What is more, the ISI had a virtual veto in its hands, given its close relations with some of the most powerful Afghan-Pashtun commanders. One of them was Jallaladin Haqqani, a man who had attracted the attention of Washington: "He was seen by CIA officers in Islamabad and others as perhaps the most impressive Pashtun battlefield commander in the war. He sponsored some of the first Arab fighters who faced Soviet forces in 1987."[5] He was a real warrior who was wounded in combat, not a virtual commander who resided in the comforts of Quetta, Baluchistan. He enjoyed close ties with Pakistan's ISI and staunch Islamists in that country, as well as wealthy Saudi sheiks. He operated in the Parrot Beak's area of Afghanistan, close to where bin Laden had his base. Although he was a bitter enemy of America, Washington provided him with a generous supply of arms and ammunition because he was such an accomplished commander.

According to Artemy Kalinovsky, the Kremlin had considered the prospects for a coalition government: "In the summer of 1988, President Zia told Vorontsov, Moscow's ambassador to Kabul, that he would support a solution in which a third of the government would be PDPA, a third would be the 'moderate' opposition, including royalists, and a third would be from the 'Peshawar Seven'."[6] That prospect, however, faded with Zia's death and also delayed an agreement, because without the steady hand of the Pakistani dictator, the opposition became an even more unruly entity.

- The United States continued to provide arms to the resistance movement long after the UN diplomatic undertaking lost steam. Washington would not accept a proposal that allowed the communists to have real influence in Kabul since they were the ones that encouraged the Soviet invasion in the first place. The United States continued to seek close ties with Pashtun commanders like Haqqani even though he was vocal in his hatred of America. Simultaneously, some in Washington considered Massoud, the charismatic Tajik commander who was Rabbani's defense minister, a more likely ally. From his base in Panjshir, he had the capacity, with Uzbek commanders, to control much of the Northern tier of the country. Like his Pashtun competitors, he too had friends among the Arabs, most notably Abdullah Assam, the Palestinian who taught bin Laden in Jeddah and whose motto was, "Jihad and the rifle alone; no negotiations, no conferences, no dialogues."[7] Given Massoud's association with drug dealing, however, he was suspect in the eyes of many in official Washington circles.
- There were serious divisions between the Afghan émigrés and the resistance fighters. Some of the most militant members of the mujahedeen resented individuals who had left Afghanistan and had only returned after the war. Others,

like Harmid Karzai, were held suspect. Even though he was a royalist because he had lived in Quetta, some of his critics deemed him an ISI agent, while others later resented his initial support of the Taliban. He was deputy foreign minister when he was interrogated and beaten by members of the government. Afterwards he left the country and did not return for 7 years.[8]

• King Zahir Shah's advanced age denied him the mental and physical capacity to play a leading role in reconciliation; besides, he was deemed unacceptable by Pakistan because he endorsed the creation of a single Pashtun state that would have united Pashtuns living on both sides of the Durand Line.

WASHINGTON'S AND MOSCOW'S FAILURE

In anticipation of Najibullah's imminent demise, it was apparent that Washington and Moscow had good cause to back moderates like Massoud and join forces in opposing the Pashtun jihadists and their Arab mentors. Indeed, one of the factors that attracted the Kremlin's attention was Massoud's success in building schools and hospitals in his area of control. But the government in Kabul would not work with him unless he surrendered his arms, and he, of course, refused to do so.[9] In the final analysis, Cold War enmity prevailed, and there was scant hope of fruitful American-Soviet cooperation on this critical matter. Fixated upon the past, the leaders in both capitals missed opportunities for future cooperation that served the vital interests of both Moscow and Washington.

It should be underlined that while the Americans had provided arms and funds to the mujahedeen, this help went through the ISI. Brigadier Mohammad Yousaf coordinated it during the war, and there was no direct American contact with the insurgents.[10] As a consequence, given this fact and the anti-American enmity among the mujahedeen, Washington might have found it difficult to influence the jihadists in this critical period, even if it had tried to do so.

Rabbani was proclaimed president in 1993, but his administration was faced with a mixture of warlords, tribal chiefs, and criminal organizations that sought power in Kabul or deemed the instability that ravaged the country in their vital interests. The civil war that tormented Afghanistan for several years cost many innocent lives. For example, in 1993 an estimated 10,000 civilians were killed as a result of fighting between Rabbani's forces and those of Hekmetyar. A year later, much of Kabul was destroyed as fighters associated with the Uzbek warlord, General Dostum, clashed with those of Hekmetyar. There were many other battles where the casualties were high, and atrocities on both sides were numerous.

It was in the crucible of this mayhem that a further step was taken toward the creation of a global Islamic terrorist movement. In a word, Afghan nationalism was fused with messianic Arab fundamentalist dogma to give rise to a movement with globalist ambitions. For example, Afghan warlord Haqqani developed close ties with the Muslim Brotherhood, and his militant brand of jihadism attracted most of the Arab fighters in Afghanistan to his side. With the exit of the Soviet forces, the Arabs would play a more important role in shaping developments within Afghanistan as would the mujahedeen and their supporters and other anti-Soviet elements from several Pakistani cities. In the Pakistani Islamic coffee shops, the Arabs would provide the intellectual framework for creating an Islamic government in Afghanistan that would adhere to fundamentalist Islamic law and practices. They also would turn their enmity away from the Union of Soviet Socialist Republics (USSR) toward the United States. In addition, Washington's support for Israel, its invasion of Iraq, and the deployment of troops on holy Islamic soil in Saudi Arabia, elevated Americans to the avant-garde of modernist values, thus threatening Islam in every corner of the globe. At the same time, Afghanistan provided a template for the Arab radicals who dreamed about creating an Islamic Caliphate throughout the Muslim world, and a strategic base from which they would wage war against those Muslim leaders that were deemed infidels or western puppets.

It is against this backdrop of events that there is some justification for the claim that, had the American and the Soviet/Russian leaders in the early 1990s cooperated in Afghanistan, it is conceivable that September 11, 2001 (9/11) might have been avoided. The alliance between the Afghan mujahedeen and Arab jihadists would not have borne fruit. It is with this thought in mind that many observers in both Washington and Moscow today favor a reset in relations and close cooperation in preventing the Taliban's return to power in Afghanistan.

Speculation of this nature aside, what we know is that the United States closed its embassy in Kabul as Afghanistan was wracked by civil war. The United States, in effect, was closing the door on the Afghan Question, but radical jihadists would soon reopen it.

ENDNOTES - CHAPTER 2

1. Diego Cordovez and Selig S. Harrison, *Out of Afghanistan,* New York: Oxford University Press, 1995, pp. 368-370.

2. Steve Coll, *Ghost Wars,* New York: Penguin Books, 2004, p. 235.

3. Artemy Kalinovsky, *A Long Goodby,* Boston, MA: Harvard University Press, 2011, p. 34.

4. Cordovez and Harrison, p. 381. Cordovez, who was the UN negotiator, indicates that if Pakistan's President Mohammed ul-Haq Zia had not been killed in a mysterious plane crash, he would have had the heft to secure an agreement among the disparate players in the Afghan drama, p. 378.

5. Coll, p. 202. Haqqani's deadliest enemy was Massoud, the Tajik, who also had displayed great courage and military acumen during his struggles with the Soviets and their Afghan allies. Perhaps the respect that he earned on the part of the Soviet commanders would pave the way for Moscow later becoming a strong supporter of the Northern Alliance. Wright, p. 95. Abullah Azzam, the Palestinian who was on good terms with the Tajik leader, sought, but without success, to resolve the dispute between Massoud and Haqqani. While they were bitter rivals, they both were devout Islamists who were strong opponents of both capitalism and communism and harbored dreams about creating a pristine Islamic state in Afghanistan.

6. Kalinovsky, p. 155.

7. Wright, p. 95.

8. Coll, pp. 286-287.

9. Kalinovsky, p. 104.

10. Peter Bergen, "Myths about Osama bin Laden," *Washington Post*, May 8, 2011.

CHAPTER 3

THE TALIBAN AND OSAMA BIN LADEN

THE ORIGINS OF THE TALIBAN

The Afghan civil war provided the strategic environment within which the Taliban emerged. It was a partnership of government deserters, former anti-Soviet mujahedeen, and young Pashtun men who were products of religious schools and Islamic grass-roots organizations that inculcated the faithful with radical jihadist dogma. These zealots gained notoriety among ordinary folk when they turned their guns against brutal criminal gangs and grasping warlords in and around the city of Kandahar. Their ranks swelled as they co-opted warlords and attracted Islamic militants to their cause as they demonstrated the capacity to crush their enemies.

They also attracted resolute support from abroad — primarily from Saudi Arabia and Pakistan. The Taliban were adherents of *Wahhabism*, an orthodox Sunni sect that imposed strict fundamentalist religious practices on the part of the faithful, so they were favored by religious allies in Saudi Arabia. In addition to generous funding to construct and operate madrassas and mosques, the Saudis provided the military equipment required to enhance the Taliban's prospects for victory in the civil war. The Saudis likewise deemed them an asset in halting the Shiite revolution that had erupted in Iran and threatened Sunni governments throughout the Islamic community. That threat had arisen after the Americans destroyed Saddam Hussein's regime in Iraq and disrupted the balance of power in the Arab Middle East. Saddam was a military threat, but so were the Islamic mullahs in Iran and, what is more, they were resolute enemies backed by the largest population in the Persian Gulf.

The key Saudi player in the Afghanistan Question was Prince Nur Mohammed Taraki, the American-educated director of Saudi Arabia's security service. Like other Saudi leaders, he feared that with the Soviet Union's collapse, the Shiite revolutionaries in Iran would spread their teachings throughout the Persian Gulf and in Central Asia. With generous assistance and sage advice from Riyadh, the pious young radicals in Taliban would sustain Sunni domination of Afghanistan. They were simple, poorly educated fanatics who might not always make wise decisions, but they would mellow over time and adopt prudent fundamentalist policies much like those that prevailed in his country.

Taraki's counterparts in Washington embraced disparate views of the Taliban; in some circles, they were deemed a positive force that could bring security to a society that had been riven by conflict for decades. In other ones, their human rights violations were a cause for alarm, e.g., their brutal mistreatment of women suggested that they were a Sunni analogue to the Shiite fanatics that ruled Iran. If anything, they were even more stringent in imposing what they claimed to be Sharia law upon the faithful.

For Pakistan, the Taliban provided the opportunity to end the Afghan civil war in a manner favorable to it. And with a friendly government in Kabul, Islamabad enjoyed strategic space that protected it against a range of enemies foreign and domestic. This meant defeating the Uzbek and Tajik warlords in the North who were receiving support from Iran, India, and Russia. Of utmost urgency, it meant installing a strong government in Kabul that was beholden to Pakistan, not to India. Likewise, the Taliban could serve as a counterweight to the Iranian Shiites that had considerable influence in Western Afghanistan, and who could make trouble for Islamabad in Baluchistan where separatists were active.

Afghanistan under Taliban control was an asset in Pakistan's campaign to pacify the unruly Pashtun tribal lands that ran along the Afghanistan-Pakistan border. One of the greatest fears harbored by Pakistani strategists was the prospect that at some point the millions of Pashtuns who lived on both sides of the Durand Line might press for an independent state of their own. The hardliners in Islamabad could not forget that because of their own ham-handed policies, they had prompted their brethren in Eastern Pakistan to break with them and create Bangladesh.

For the most part, the U.S. foreign policy community remained indifferent to the developments that were unfolding in Afghanistan. The only official American-Taliban meeting that took place occurred in April 1998. Bill Richardson, the U.S. Ambassador to the UN, flew to Kabul with the intention of meeting with Mullah Omar in an effort to persuade him to hand over bin Laden to the Saudis in keeping with a UN resolution that had condemned the al-Qaeda leader. Richardson neither met with Omar nor did he succeed in getting the Taliban to return bin Laden to Saudi Arabia.[1]

Halting Soviet aggression was the original rationale for U.S. involvement in Afghanistan, which proved to be a disaster for Moscow, helping expedite the implosion of the Soviet regime. Consequently, the George H. W. Bush, Bill Clinton, and George W. Bush administrations lost interest in the country, failing to develop a coherent response to the stormy events that were unfolding in Afghanistan. Among other things, President George H. W. Bush closed the U.S. Embassy in Kabul.[2]

Meanwhile, within Afghanistan the educated middle class was alarmed by the Taliban's zeal and puritanical policies. After all, it was monstrous that girls no longer could attend school while men had to grow beards and adhere to puritanical behavior that was both irrational and demeaning, not to mention the Taliban's barbaric acts of punishment. A Taliban victory meant Afghanistan was returning to the Middle Ages. Something else of significance was occurring: as religious zealots gained power, the influence of the tribes and their leaders was marginalized. This worked in behalf of the radical jihadists that soon would embrace the fantasies of their Arab benefactors.

For ordinary folk, the Taliban's harsh policies were often deemed excessive, but after years of turmoil, many Afghans looked upon the religious zealots with favor. Where they ruled, people could enjoy both order and peace, and they relished the Taliban's making quick work of thieves and rapacious warlords who had brutalized them for years. And in most instances, if one did not challenge them, the Taliban would leave him or her alone.

Steve Coll provides another reason for their favorable reception among Pashtun leaders. In the crucible of war, Afghan nationalism and Islamic piety were forged into a powerful weapon. More to the point, by combining Islamic piety with Pashtun political heft, the Taliban provided the Pashtun tribes with the potential to end the civil war and gain control of the government in Kabul.[3] This is why many prominent

Pashtun elders and tribal chiefs, including those associated with the royalist Karzai family, supported the radical jihadists.

After several years of civil war, powerful religious and secular Pashtun leaders and commercial oligarchs lost patience with the marauding warlords that had torn the country asunder. They sought an end to the violence that not only devastated their pocketbooks, but at times even cost them their lives. As a consequence, a growing number of them threw their weight behind a cabal of young mullahs who led the Taliban.

Under the leadership of a cleric called Mullah Mohammed Omar, the Taliban became a capable fighting force and a social-political reform movement that was committed to a peaceful and unified Afghanistan. Omar was something of a recluse who avoided publicity, but he had lost an eye fighting the Soviets and was no stranger to organized violence. He was born in 1950 in a village outside of Kandahar, with that ancient Pashtun city, which he rarely left, becoming his base. After the Soviet War, he returned to his religious studies and characterized his associates as "a simple band of dedicated youths determined to establish the laws of God on Earth and prepared to sacrifice everything in pursuit of that goal."[4]

After capturing Kandahar in 1994, the Taliban secured a growing number of provinces where they were greeted as saviors by a war-weary, largely Pashtun population. Confident of gaining control of the entire country, Omar refused to negotiate with his enemies or did so only for tactical reasons. When asked what he would do with his enemies, he answered bluntly, "Kill them."

In September 1994, Herat fell to the Taliban and, with that victory, Omar's fighters occupied the entire southern tier of Afghanistan from the east to the west. The Hazara Shiite population, however, suffered under the fanatical rule of their Sunni masters who committed numerous atrocities. After every success, they attracted a steady stream of students from Pakistan's madrassas to replenish their ranks but, as they entered the Northern half of the country, they encountered stiff resistance from Uzbek and Tajik militias and Shiite fighters. Nonetheless, in May 1997 they secured control of Mazar-i-Sharif, the largest city in Northern Afghanistan. It had a reputation of urbane secularism and was controlled by Dostum, "a former communist general who wore his religion lightly."[5]

Soon after the Taliban expelled his forces and occupied the city, the local population rebelled and killed many of the occupiers. Here was further evidence that the Taliban's enemies in the North would prove to be tough and resourceful fighters. In turn, the Taliban engaged in awful human rights crimes, indiscriminately killing civilians and warriors alike in the conviction that anyone who resisted them or who did not join them was an enemy of God, of Islam.

The Taliban's victory in Mazar had international implications because it provided Pakistan, Saudi Arabia, and the United Arab Emirates with the rationale for extending diplomatic recognition to them. The Taliban, however, were rejected by most of the international community.

One rationale for withholding diplomatic recognition was that a northern tier of Afghanistan remained outside of the Taliban's control. The major reason for this was the existence of fighters who were led by the Tajik warlord, Massoud, by far their most gifted opponent. His fighters represented the last source of significant military opposition to the Taliban, and his resistance was made possible by arms, equipment, and money received from India, Iran, and Russia. According to one report, since the Taliban had indicated that the Central Asian countries and Russia itself would be a target of their Islamic crusade, the Kremlin had deployed 28,000 Russian troops to outposts in Central Asia. It was from these areas that most of the equipment that sustained Massoud's fighters originated.

His Russian benefactors, however, had to know that Massoud bankrolled his movement by dealing in heroin, most of which was used by addicts in Russia.[6] Moscow had no alternative since he was the last remaining military barrier standing between the Taliban and Central Asia. With help from foreign sources, he maintained a force that became known as the Northern Alliance and that would provide the United States with the boots on the ground in 2001 to expel the Taliban from Afghanistan.

It would take some time before Massoud felt comfortable with the United States, and Washington with him. He concluded that the Americans were allied with Pakistan and had endorsed the ISI's pro-Taliban tilt. What is more, he saw the U.S. energy company Unocal's campaign to build a pipeline from Turkmenistan through Afghanistan to Pakistan as evidence that powerful oil interests in America were lobbying their government to court the Taliban.

OSAMA BIN LADEN

Meanwhile, American intelligence noted with dismay that the Taliban had secured a close relationship with foreign fighters associated with a Saudi millionaire called Osama bin Laden. In their drive toward Kabul in 1996, they captured Jalalabad where bin Laden had grown roots since he left Sudan. He would develop a close personal relationship with Mullah Omar and marry one of his daughters. Like some of the other Arabs in his circle, bin Laden was filling Omar with grand notions about global jihad. The Taliban's link with him was one of the factors that would eventually result in the United States looking to Massoud with greater favor.

The Taliban would never defeat Massoud on the battlefield, but it captured Kabul in 1996 and took control of the government. With the Taliban victory, we see a clear path between the 1979 Soviet invasion of Afghanistan, the civil war that followed the USSR's humiliating exit, and the U.S. intervention 21 years later that was precipitated by September 11, 2001 (9/11). The connecting link between the Taliban victory and that monstrous event, of course, was bin Laden himself.

After working for Aramco as a carpenter, Osama bin Laden's Yemini father, Muhammed, evenually became owner and operator of the largest construction company in Saudi Arabia. Much of Aramco's infrastructure would be built by his companies. In the process, he became a close associate of the King and a significant force in Saudi society. Osama, one of his father's many children, would become a devout Muslim and in high school joined the Muslim Brothers, a radical underground organization that hoped someday to establish an Islamic state. He attended King Abdul Aziz University in Jeddah where many of his instructors were Islamists.

After the Soviet invasion of Afghanistan, bin Laden was enthralled by the accounts of the mujahedeen provided by one of his mentors, Sheikh Abdullah Azzam. The Palestinian cleric was a prominent personality in his own right among Islamic radicals, for, among other things, he ordered a fatwa that obliged Muslims to fight the Soviet infidels in Afghanistan. He would later be assassinated under mysterious circumstances, and some would say his death was a result of internal upheaval among the jihadists. Many Arabs had been attracted to Azzam's fatwa—Defense of Muslim Lands—stating that Muslims were obligated to fight for their Islamic brothers against the infidels in Afghanistan. No more than 3,000 Arab fighters were recruited through the Afghan Services Bureau that Azzam created and bin Laden bankrolled; indeed, many of them never entered the war zone.[7]

Eventually, bin Laden led Arabs in a number of battles and, as a consequence, earned the reputation of being a warrior as well as a generous financial benefactor of the mujahedeen. After Soviet forces left Afghanistan in humiliation, he returned to his homeland in 1989, and Turki asked for his help in organizing "a fundamentalist religion-based resistance to the Communist-style regime in South Yemen." But by this time, bin Laden was enthralled with the idea of striking the United States, Islam's most powerful enemy.[8] He had not, however, altogether forgotten the "near enemy." For example, he told the Saudi leaders, "I want to fight Saddam, an infidel. I want to establish a guerrilla war against Iraq."[9]

Relations between bin Laden and the Saudi government would decline when, in a meeting with Dick Cheney, the King agreed to deploy a large number of U.S. troops and weapon systems in the kingdom to expel Saddam from Kuwait. The King feared that the Iraqi dictator, if not punished for his invasion and occupation of Kuwait, might decide to cross the border and remove the Saudi leadership from power. Bin

Laden did not immediately break with the King, even though he was outraged that Americans were treading on holy Saudi soil and feared that, once deployed, they would never leave the country. He sustained his Afghanistan Services Bureau, a front for maintaining the network of Algerians, Chechens, Egyptians, and other Muslims who had fought in Afghanistan. After the Soviet Union collapsed, many of these fighters would join their brethren to fight in Chechnya and the Balkans. In 1990, he founded an organization that in a decade would become a household name, al-Qaeda.[10]

As late as 1993, however, neither bin Laden nor his new organization were broached in conversations conducted by the CIA and the Federal Bureau of Investigation (FBI) in their investigations of the World Trade Center bombing that year. This was true even though one of the individuals arrested for this attack, El Sayyid Nosair, had materials in his New York apartment connecting him to the Afghan Services Bureau. It was not realized at the time, but he would be the first al-Qaeda terrorist arrested in the United States. He and several other plotters, including the blind Egyptian cleric, Omar Abdel Rahman, would be apprehended as well; but the leader of the terrorist crew, Ramzi Yousef, would flee the country. In 1995, he was foiled in a plot to place bombs on U.S. airliners flying from Asia. Soon afterwards, he was spotted in Pakistan and was snatched by a team of American intelligence operatives with the help of Pakistani colleagues and returned to the United States.

Bin Laden's incessant criticism of the Saudi government and anti-American vitriol resulted in mounting pressure upon him at home, so he relocated to Sudan where he was welcomed by Hasan al-Turabi, the radical Islamist leader. In Sudan, bin Laden continued to pursue his jihadist activities and, as a consequence of them and his blistering rhetorical attacks upon the Saudi leaders and their American friends, he was asked to leave the country.[11]

By late 1994, the CIA concluded that he was a direct threat to the United States, and not just a financier of terrorist organizations.[12] He left Sudan for Afghanistan, proclaiming that the United States was responsible for his deportation. It is believed that he was introduced to Omar by ISI agents, although bin Laden obviously had many contacts of his own in Afghanistan and perhaps the first meeting was just one of happenstance. But one thing is clear—he became a generous benefactor of the Taliban, along with other wealthy Arabs. He also became a close associate of Omar, although earlier the Taliban leader had promised Tareki that he would hand over bin Laden if the Saudis made the request. Omar later denied ever doing so. It was from a cave in Afghanistan in 1996 that bin Laden would declare war on the United States through a fatwa prompted by American forces remaining in Saudi Arabia, 5 years after the First Gulf War ended.[13]

THE UNITED STATES ACKNOWLEDGES BIN LADEN AS A THREAT

By this time, Richard Clarke, the White House terrorist expert, and his colleagues knew a lot about bin Laden and his close relationship with the Taliban. On February 23, 1998, bin Laden announced the formation of a coalition, the International Islamic Front for Jihad Against Jews and Crusaders.[14] Henceforth, he would recruit fighters from throughout the Umma with the explicit purpose in mind of punishing Islam's greatest enemy, the United States of America.

Upon his return to Afghanistan, he developed a close relationship with Ayman Zawahiri, an Egyptian physician who had been arrested and tortured by his captors in his home country for his subversive activities. The leader of a group called Islamic Jihad, Zawahiri sought a sanctuary to continue his revolutionary activities in Afghanistan and to secure financial support for his movement. Some presumed that this led him to befriend bin Laden since the Saudi had the cash to help Zawahiri bankroll his flagging organization.

In the 1980s, Zawahiri served the jihadist cause in Afghanistan where he had worked for the Red Crescent. But his agenda was global in scope, for he saw the struggle in Afghanistan as "a training course of the utmost importance to prepare the Muslim mujahedeen to wage their awaited battle against the superpower that now has sole dominance over the globe, namely, the United States."[15]

At the same time, Zawahiri was an exponent of *takfir*, the Arab word for excommunication. In the eyes of modern advocates of this doctrine, anyone who adheres to anti-Islamic ideas like democracy is an infidel. "Democracy . . .was against Islam because it placed in the hands of people authority that properly belonged to God."[16] *Takfir* was interpreted by the radicals who formed al-Qaeda as giving license to the killing of anyone who aided or abetted infidels. It was with just such venomous thoughts in mind that those Muslim leaders who were allied with the West, the hated Americans in particular, would become targets of jihadists. They were deemed the "near enemy." They had to be destroyed by the jihadists along with the "far enemy," the Americans.

It is noteworthy, however, that such callous attitudes towards the murder of fellow human beings had resulted in a significant reversal for Zawahiri and his radical followers in Egypt. On November 17, 1997, they massacred 58 tourists and 4 Egyptians at the resort city of Luxor in an attempt to strike at the country's prized tourist industry and to advance violence as a legitimate jihadist tool.[17] The people of Egypt were shocked, and the attack proved to be a devastating setback for Zawahiri and his fanatical followers.

The Egyptian physician and the Saudi millionaire had something else in common; they were both admirers of Sayyid Qutb, the Egyptian jihadist thinker who was one of the first to turn Islamic jihadism against the disruptions and values embedded in a modern world that has its roots in Western civilization. The reserved bookish man spent time in the United States after World War II and became radicalized as a result of the experience. Qutb's

> central concern was modernity. Modern values— secularism, rationality, democracy, subjectivity, individualism, mixing of the sexes, tolerance, and materialism—had infected Islam through the agency of Western colonialism. America now stood for all that. Qutb's polemic was directed at Egyptians who wanted to bend Islam around the modern world. He intended to show that Islam and modernity were completely incompatible.

What is more, "Separation of the sacred and the secular state and religion, science and theology, mind and spirit—these were the hallmarks of modernity, which had captured the West. But Islam could not abide such divisions."[18]

All of bin Laden's mentors were familiar with Qutb's writings and lamented his execution by Egyptian authorities for revolting against the government.

As he had hoped, his death catapulted him into the Pantheon of Islamic martyrs. Bin Laden never met the man but in developing a close personal relationship with Zawahiri, he found a fellow admirer of Qutb. In keeping with Qutb's worldview, Zawahiri deemed the Western-dominated global system a cancer that imperiled Muslims everywhere; therefore, it had to be excised by any means necessary. Of course, America was the system's dominant actor and like bin Laden, Zawahiri pondered how the United States — as with the USSR — could be enticed into the killing fields of Afghanistan.

According to Lawrence Wright, this was the rationale for the October 12, 2000, bombing of the USS *Cole* anchored in Aden Harbor. Afterward, bin Laden became the premier leader in the eyes of those jihadists who travelled to his training camp in Afghanistan in the hope of becoming martyrs. But the expected retaliation did not come, as the Clinton administration was preoccupied with the Israeli-Palestinian peace talks and a presidential election.

> Bin Laden was angry and disappointed. He hoped to lure America into the same trap the Soviets had fallen into: Afghanistan. His strategy was to continually attack until the U.S. forces invaded; then the mujahedeen would swarm upon them and bleed them until the entire American empire fell from its wounds.

The attack on the U.S. embassies in Africa had failed, and now the same thing happened with the insult to the USS *Cole*. "He would have to create an irresistible outrage."[19]

By this time, bin Laden was no longer perceived merely as a Taliban moneyman but as their active ally in jihadist violence. He was the man responsible for the first attack against the twin towers in Manhattan and other terrorist strikes such as the killing of CIA personnel outside its Northern Virginia headquarters and the bombings of two U.S. embassies in Kenya and Tanzania, as well as the killing of 17 sailors on the USS *Cole*.

After the African attacks, the Taliban pledged to protect him, prompting a U.S. cruise missile strike on camps in Jalalabad and Khost. They resulted in 21 people killed and 30 wounded. The Clinton administration resisted subsequent opportunities to kill bin Laden, concluding that too many civilians would be put at risk in the contemplated strikes. For the U.S. national security community at large, the issue of terrorism remained a side show.

Bin Laden was training thousands of terrorists, and the Taliban's refusal to hand him over to an international tribunal indicated that they were complicit in the global jihadist movement. After the U.S. 2000 election, the outgoing security officials in the Clinton administration warned the incoming government that terrorism would represent the greatest threat to U.S. security. Even more to the point, these warnings from Richard Clarke, the White House terrorist expert, and George Tenet, the CIA director, asserted that an al-Qaeda attack against the United States was imminent. Their warnings were dismissed.

The Bush White House would not preoccupy itself with "global terrorism" until after the deadly strikes on the World Trade Center and the Pentagon on that fateful 9/11 day. Peter Bergen described the situation as follows:

> Over the course of the coming weeks and months, the Bush administration would set the course of policies

that would have unforeseen consequences for many years into the future: a "light footprint" operation in Afghanistan, which would succeed brilliantly at toppling the Taliban, but leave many of the top leaders of al-Qaeda at liberty following the failure to capture or kill them at the battle of Tora Bora in December 2001, and would also fail to secure Afghanistan for the long term. Bush also launched the nation on an ambiguous and open-ended conflict against a tactic, termed the "war on terror," which would warp U.S. foreign policy and distort key American ideals about the rule of law, while his administration's obsession with Iraq would lead the United States into fighting two wars in the Muslim world simultaneously, seeming to confirm one of bin Laden's key claims — "the West, led by America, was at war with Islam."[20]

ENDNOTES - CHAPTER 3

1. For a discussion of the Richardson trip, see Bruce Riedel, *Deadly Embrace*, Washington, DC: The Brookings Institution, 2011, p. 45.

2. Steve Coll, in his masterful book, *Ghost Wars*, blames both Clinton and his Republican predecessors for lacking the political vision to take decisive action in Afghanistan to subvert the Taliban. Those who were associated with Massoud, like Karzai, were deemed bit players or inept self-promoters like Abdul Haq, while the Taliban had the support of Jallaldin Haqqani, who was a favorite of the CIA during the war against the Soviets. At the same time, many Afghan watchers in the government deemed the anti-Taliban Pashtun groups disorganized and incapable of mounting serious opposition to Mullah Omar and his supporters. The knowledge that Massoud was running drugs, of course, hardly burnished his image among American officials, either.

3. *Ibid.*, p. 283.

4. *Ibid.*, p. 289.

5. *Ibid.*, p. 348.

6. *Ibid.*, p. 345.

7. Lawrence Wright described the Arab suicide bombers in the following terms:

> The lure of an illustrious and meaningful death was especially powerful in cases where the pleasures and rewards of life were crushed by government oppression and economic deprivation. From Iraq to Morocco, Arab governments had stifled freedom and signally failed to create wealth at the very time when democracy and personal income were sharply climbing in virtually all other parts of the globe . . . if one subtracted the oil revenues in the Gulf countries, 260 million Arabs exported less than the 5 million Finns.

See his *The Looming Tower*, New York: Alfred A. Knopf, 2006, p. 107.

8. Richard A. Clarke, *Against All Enemies: Inside America's War on Terror*, New York: Free Press, 2004, p. 59.

9. Coll, p. 222.

10. Al-Qaeda's efforts to lend assistance to fellow Muslims in the Balkans began early in 1992, and the Arab fighters proved to be brutal and effective in engaging the Serbs.

11. What is more, there were radical jihadists in Sudan that questioned bin Laden's religious piety. On one occasion during 1994, an attempt was made to assassinate him in a Khartoum mosque. See Coll, p. 269.

12. In a message to the Americans, bin Laden warned, "Terrorizing you, while you are carrying arms in our land, is a legitimate right and a moral obligation." Then addressing the U.S. Secretary of Defense William Perry, he continued, "I say to you, William, that these youths [al-Qaeda fighters] love death as you love life. These youths will not ask for explanations. They will sing out that there is nothing between us that needs to be explained, there is only killing and neck-smiting." See Wright, p. 4.

13. Coll, p. 380. The group stated that the United States had declared war on Allah and the signatories of the document "hereby give all Muslims the following judgment: The judgment to kill and fight Americans and their allies, whether civilians or military, is an obligation for every Muslim who is able to do so in any country."

14. Wright, p. 46.

15. *Ibid.*, p. 124. For a more recent discussion of bin Laden, see Peter L. Bergen, *The Longest War*, New York: Free Press, 2011.

16. Wright, pp. 256-257.

17. *Ibid.*, p. 24. In the aftermath of bin Laden's death, close watchers of al-Qaeda assumed, correctly, that Zawahiri would fill the leader's shoes.

18. *Ibid.*, p. 331.

19. *Ibid.*

20. Bergen, p. 52.

CHAPTER 4

9/11 AND WAR AGAINST THE TALIBAN AND AL-QAEDA

THE SEPTEMBER 2001 TERRORIST ATTACKS

On the morning of September 12, 2001, Richard Clarke, the manager of the NSC's Counterterrorism Security Group, spoke to Paul Wolfowitz regarding who was to blame for September 11, 2001 (9/11). Defense Secretary Donald Rumsfeld's second in command was not convinced that al-Qaeda was behind the attacks since it was too sophisticated to be conducted by a cabal of terrorists. A state had to be responsible for them, and that state was Iraq. Rumsfeld was of the same opinion, and he consistently talked about "getting Iraq." In an evening conversation with the President at the White House situation room, Bush said to Clarke, "Look, I know you have a lot to do and all . . . but I want you, as soon as you can, to go back over everything. See if Saddam did this. See if he's linked in any way. . . ." Clarke was "taken aback" and said, "But, Mr. President, al-Qaeda did this." He added that the anti-terrorist analysts in the government had looked and found no connection between bin Laden and Iraq or any other state. "'Look into Iraq, Saddam,' the President said testily and left us."[1]

A week later, Clarke sent a memo to the National Security Council (NSC) Director Condoleezza Rice titled, "Survey of International Information of Any Iraqi Involvement in the September 11 Attack." It concluded there was "no complicity" on Iraq's part.[2] The next day, Rumsfeld gave orders for a plan to be devised to invade the southern oil fields of Iraq. They were issued even before we as a nation had decided what to do about Afghanistan![3] In Peter Bergen's words that deserve to be repeated, this was a fateful error, for

> Bush . . . launched the nation on an ambiguous and open-ended conflict against a tactic, termed the 'war on terror,' which would warp U.S. foreign policy and distort key American ideals about the rule of law, while his administration's obsession with Iraq would lead the United States into fighting two wars in the Muslim world simultaneously, seeming to confirm one of bin Laden's key claims — that the West, led by America, was at war with Islam.[4]

In sum, the administration had been contemplating regime change in Iraq for some time, and Afghanistan, however justified, was a mere sideshow.

Of course, those responsible for 9/11 in Afghanistan had to be brought to justice and, toward this end, the Bush administration demanded that the Taliban hand over bin Laden for prosecution (the Iraq invasion, therefore, had to be put on hold). Initially bin Laden told Mullah Omar that he was innocent of the charge, but later he proudly conceded that he was responsible for the attack. When the truth was revealed and the U.S. retaliatory strike began, many members of the Taliban leadership "were outraged at bin Laden's abuse of their hospitality and his blatant disregard for their government." But, "the combative international stance towards the Taliban, the polarization of the Islamic world, and the fear of Mohammad Omar and others of losing the few allies they believed they had left, pushed them into a de facto defense of bin Laden."[5] Thus when Omar's colleagues urged him to hand over bin Laden to the international community to be tried, he said no.

It is alleged that when contemplating the U.S. military response—what would become known as Operation ENDURING FREEDOM—"Pakistani security officials assured the inexperienced leader [i.e., Omar] that the United States would react in a limited way, as in 1998 following the African bombings of U.S. embassies."[6] Ignorant of the world outside of Afghanistan, Omar and his associates were once again manipulated by foreigners—previously by al-Qaeda and at this point in time by the ISI. Bergen asserts that there was no evidence that bin Laden anticipated that the United States would respond by invading Afghanistan. Here was a further example of the al-Qaeda leader's wishful thinking and flawed understanding.[7]

On September 12, 2001, the UN Security Council passed a resolution authorizing the use of force against terrorists, and that same day NATO invoked Article Five in a demonstration of solidarity with the United States. Two days later, the U.S. Congress endorsed an Authorization for Use of Military Force against "those nations, organization, or persons" that planned or committed terrorist attacks against the United States.[8] President Bush addressed the American people on September 20 and shared with them his interpretation of the rationale behind the attacks and how he would respond to them. He stated that those responsible for 9/11 hated us and our freedom. As a consequence, we would wage war against al-Qaeda but, "It will not end until every terrorist group of global reach has been defeated."[9]

ROUTING THE JIHADISTS

After it became clear that Saddam neither had nuclear weapons nor had he collaborated with al-Qaeda, some supporters of the invasion portrayed the jihadists as 21st century analogues of Hitler and Stalin. But both these men had truly awesome military forces at their command and were responsible for the death of tens of millions of people and horrendous physical destruction. By contrast, "the war on terrorism" today has caused deaths in the thousands and modest material damage.

In an attempt to justify the Iraq War, the President and influential analysts outside of the government grossly distorted the capacity of the enemy. Consequently, they failed to answer the most elementary question facing military strategists: "What is the nature of the enemy?" That question became entangled in the Bush administration's campaign to justify a war of choice, not necessity. In the process, discourse bearing on critical national security issues became entangled in an Orwellian universe of deceit, deception, and disinformation. Under these circumstances, it became extremely difficult to conduct an objective discussion of the war in Iraq. That environment persists to this day in some circles and has diminished serious discourse bearing on our operations in Afghanistan.

Meanwhile, in the enemy camp, and in keeping with their illusions of grandeur, the Taliban were ill-prepared to resist the military tsunami that was coming their way. They and their allies thought they would defeat the Americans just as they did the Soviets. Their morale, however, plunged after being crushed by the joint American-Northern Federation onslaught.

With its air power monopoly, the United States struck any and all Taliban targets that could provide its fighters with the infrastructure for combat. That included its small air force and airfields, anti-aircraft units, and other communications and logistical targets of any significance. The trouble was that Pentagon planners found very little to strike. On the ground, the Special Forces, with our British cousins and the Northern Alliance troops, proved superior to their adversaries and made quick work of the enemy. Those that were not captured or killed, returned home or fled to Pakistan. In the end, a significant number of the "Arab-Afghans" that did not seek a safe harbor there left the region altogether and sought jihad in Bosnia, Somalia, Russia, and Yemen.

In addition to evoking Article Five of the Rome Treaty, the NATO-led International Assistance Force (ISAF) was created under UN auspices. Some units were deployed only to support NATO combat troops or engage in humanitarian operations. For example, the German units were deployed in the north where it was assumed the local Tajiks and Uzbeks would continue to reject the largely Pashtun Taliban. There would be little fighting, then, in their areas.

The Northern Alliance would provide the lion's share of the boots on the ground, but their successes against the Taliban and al-Qaeda were substantially bolstered by U.S. airpower and the skillful leadership of the combined CIA-Pentagon special forces teams — the Jawbreakers — that infiltrated into Afghanistan from Uzbekistan and Tajikistan. Access to the country from the south was still exceedingly difficult, given the local population's hostility, the presence of jihadist fighters, and the absence of significant anti-Taliban allies.

The Northern Alliance forces that controlled about 15 percent of Afghanistan were under the command of General Mohammad Fahim who replaced Massoud after he was assassinated by al-Qaeda agents posing as TV journalists. Massoud, on the eve of 9/11 and in a replay of his 1980s recovery against the Soviets, had designed a plan to defeat the Taliban.[10] He intended to avoid direct confrontation with the main Taliban force and to leap-frog over them, and through rapid strikes divide and demoralize them as he joined forces with his allies in disparate parts of the country. They would emerge as the fortunes of the Taliban declined. In 2001, the course of events would be in keeping with his expectations.

Estimates of the Northern Alliance troops ranged from a low of 10,000 to a high of 30,000, although Condoleezza Rice had accepted a total of 20,000 as likely.[11] They faced an enemy that numbered an estimated 40,000 to 50,000; approximately 8,000 to 12,000 of that number were foreign—mostly Arab fighters. U.S. planners assumed that the Taliban would continue to rely upon recruits from Pakistan to bolster their ranks, but it was believed that after the Afghan insurgents experienced the hammer blows of U.S. airpower, many would return home. Other pro-Taliban warlords or those sitting on the sidelines would join the Northern Alliance and its American allies.

For the most part, and in contrast to the war against the Soviets, the Taliban defenders displayed poor morale and failed to perform as well as their Arab brethren. In keeping with the practice of warriors in Afghanistan, when the odds began to shift in the adversary's favor, many tough but pragmatic mujahedeen changed sides. This happened on a number of occasions during the 2001 war, but the foreign fighters were not among this group. They fought well and were not afraid to close with their enemies, including the American troops; on the contrary, they welcomed such confrontations. In most instances, however, these showdowns did not work in their behalf because the

Americans enjoyed air superiority and possessed lethal precision-guided munitions that slaughtered the Taliban and Arab fighters alike. It is estimated that about 5,000 Taliban and their allies died, mostly from air strikes.[12]

In recognition of their superior fighting skills and blasé attitude toward death, the Arab jihadists were assigned to the most critical fronts in the war. Unlike their Afghan comrades, they had received military training and comported themselves as professional soldiers. Indeed, they had eagerly anticipated the day that they could kill Americans.

> In Operation ANACONDA [designed to capture or kill bin Laden, Zawahiri, and Omar], al Qaeda defenders not only stood their ground against overwhelming American firepower, they actually reinforced their positions in the midst of the battle: their fighters were willing to advance into the teeth of a fierce bombardment to enter the Shah-i-kot Valley from safer positions elsewhere and seek battle with our forces.[13]

After the allies achieved victories in the north, including Kabul, they moved south and, in the process, the peasant-warriors associated with the Taliban demonstrated greater resolve on the battlefield. Since most of them were Pashtun, they were now fighting under the watchful eyes of family, neighbors, and kinfolk. Still they remained vulnerable to airpower directed at them from a small number of American/allied spotters, and their ranks were devastated with powerful precision-guided munitions.

Once the war planners turned their attention to destroying the Taliban government that harbored al-Qaeda, victory occurred in a matter of weeks. At the same time, under pressure from Washington, Pakistan president Pervez Musharraf withdrew both his diplomatic and military support from them, even though it was apparent that the ISI provided the Taliban help up until the final days of the fighting.

Within the war zone, the Americans faced a serious problem of balancing ethnic frictions among its allies. The Tajiks and Uzbeks were a dominant force in the Northern Alliance, and the Hazara Shiites were similarly ascendant in Western Afghanistan around the ancient city of Herat. In the south, Pashtun leader Hamid Karzai would organize a fighting force from that dominant ethnic group. Clearly, there were profound concerns in Washington about sectarian fissures that had led to chaos in the past. In this connection, it was hoped that the disparate tribes would join Karzai, but they remained independent entities whose behavior was unpredictable.

With the outcome obvious, some Taliban leaders considered the prospect of reconciliation with the Karzai government but those who had inflicted a crushing defeat on them had little interest in working with such a spent radical force. "Similarly in 2002, Jalaluddin Haqqani's brother, Ibrahim, came to Kabul to meet with American and Afghan government officials to inquire about this possibility." According to Van Linschoten and Kuehn: "He was detained and allegedly mistreated."[14] One would be hard pressed to weep over his treatment, but perhaps an opportunity to secure the support of some jihadists for the new government had been missed.

According to two close observers of the Taliban, this was unfortunate because if they had been given the opportunity to reconcile with Karzai, the war that the United States is fighting in Afghanistan today might have been avoided. "The political process established by the Bonn Agreement of December 2001 was intended, at least by its UN sponsors, to provide a mechanism for integrating Taliban who agreed to become lawful participations." While hiding in Pakistan, the Taliban discussed the prospects of "joining the political process" but "these discussions came [to] too little."[15]

In spite of the brilliant U.S. military victory in Afghanistan, critics confronted the administration with the question: "Why did we fail to get bin Laden?" Bergen provides a number of answers: bin Laden and his people knew the area very well, and we did not; our Afghan allies were incompetent and corrupt; the Pakistanis did not provide any help; and General Franks pointed out among other things that military operations would have been interrupted had we pursued such a quarry. Furthermore, it was unclear where he was located.[16] Equally important, the local people had been devastated by U.S. air attacks, and many of them admired their al-Qaeda brethren and deemed them "holy warriors." Consequently, in keeping with Mao's metaphor, the Pashtun peasants provided an ocean within which the jihadists could escape their enemies.

Some of them could be "rented" by plying them with development dollars, but they could not be "bought" for long. Even Afghans who found the Taliban's rule excessively harsh could not ignore the trenchant fact that "the Taliban are our people, these are our boys fighting the latest wave of infidels that are entering our villages and forcing us to bow to them and to adopt alien ideas and practices." The Taliban aside, many of the people who fought the "foreigners" were men adhering to powerful tribal loyalties, and traditional notions about manhood that had nothing to do with the preaching of the Arabs who had come to fight with them.

Preoccupied with deposing Saddam Hussein, the Bush administration ignored developments in Afghanistan soon after the Taliban were routed. Washington continued to devote considerable resources to achieving bin Laden's capture or death, but he and Mullah Omar found a refuge in Pakistan's Federally Administered Tribal Areas (FATA), and so did many of their followers. There, they licked their wounds and prepared to resume jihad. They could do so in relative peace since some elements in the ISI provided them with protection and the resources to restore their fighting capability.

THE KARZAI GOVERNMENT

With the allied victory in sight, there was the matter of creating a new Afghan government. Some Northern Alliance commanders who would have played a key part in doing so no longer were available—most notably Ahmad Shah Massoud. Consequently, the man who would play a pivotal role in the new government was Hamid Karzai, a Pashtun from a prominent Afghani family whose father had been assassinated in 1999. A favorite of Washington, he had entered the country with the help of U.S. special forces, and attracted a number of Pashtun fighters to his side when Karzai's fellow Pashtuns concluded that the Americans not only supported him but would use their military prowess to crush the Taliban. He escaped death during a friendly fire mishap—the first of many occasions when he did so—and on December 22, 2001, he was sworn in as the head of the 30-member interim government. In June 2002, a *Loya Jirga*, or grand council, chose him as the head of state. He would function in that capacity until 2004 when an election to select the country's future leaders would be conducted. After a new constitution was crafted in October-November 2004, he was elected president by 55 percent of the electorate.[17]

At this point, the U.S. Government could take some comfort in the fact that while developments in Iraq had become problematic, they were looking up in Afghanistan. Some observers noted that by the crushing of the Taliban, the country that benefited most was Iran. Later, the mullahs would receive a second gift from Bush when he deposed their most feared enemy — Saddam Hussein.

In October 2001, members of the NSC and State Department met covertly with Iranian representatives in Paris and Geneva in discussions sponsored by Lakhdar Brahimi, who headed the UN Assistance Mission in Afghanistan. James Dobbins, the U.S. special envoy to Afghanistan, quarterbacked the American team. As Trita Parsai reveals,

> The talks progressed better than expected. The discussions focused on "how to effectively unseat the Taliban and once the Taliban was gone, how to stand up an Afghanistan government." The Iranian diplomats impressed their American and European counterparts tremendously with their knowledge and expertise about Afghanistan and the Taliban. And Iran's help was not negligible. The Iranians offered their air bases to the United States, they offered to perform search and rescue missions for downed American pilots, they served as a bridge between the Northern Alliance and the United States, in the fight against the Taliban, and on occasion they even used U.S. information to find and kill fleeing al-Qaeda leaders.[18]

Recognizing the value of cooperating with the Tehran, the U.S. State Department took the initiative. Secretary Colin Powell had prepared a secret comprehensive package of carrots on a stick to offer the Iranians. Unlike the Pentagon, the State Department favored a strategic opening to Iran, not just tactical discussions. The American diplomats realized that the cooperation over Afghanistan could be extended to cover al-Qaeda and other terrorist organizations. The United States and Iran could expand their intelligence-sharing cooperation and coordinate more robust border sweeps to capture al-Qaeda fighters who were fleeing into Pakistan and Iran.[19]

However, according to Colonel Lawrence Wilkerson, Powell's chief of staff, President Bush was dissuaded by Vice-President Dick Cheney and Defense Secretary Rumsfeld from supporting the idea.[20]

Tehran's diplomats were very active in the Bonn Conference of December 2001 when Karzai was selected under UN auspices. When the Iranian Deputy Foreign Minister Mohammad Javad Zarif was asked about him, he responded, "He lived in Iran for a while and we think well of him."[21] At the same time, "Iran's political clout with the various warring Afghan groups proved to be crucial; it was Iran's influence over the Afghans and not America's threats and promises that moved the negotiations forward." One of the roadblocks to an agreement emerged when representatives of the Northern Alliance refused to budge on their demand that they be given 18 of the 24 ministry posts in the new government, even though they represented only 40 percent of the country. It was only after the Iranian lead negotiator, Javad Zarif, intervened with Yunus Qanooni — the Alliance's lead representative — that he was induced to modify his demands.[22]

In addition to their diplomatic help, the Iranians had provided money and military hardware to the Northern Alliance which was especially critical in Western Afghanistan in the area surrounding Herat where Shiites lived in great numbers. Their man in Western Afghanistan was Ismail Khan, who was an ethnic Tajik and Shite. While most officials in Washington did not want to admit it, without Iran's help the stabilization of Afghanistan would have been far more difficult. Further cooperation with Iran was foreclosed when the leaders in Tehran and Washington proved incapable of setting aside their mutual animosity and fears to reestablish a relationship, even if imperfect, that could have been useful in the years ahead.

OSAMA BIN LADEN AND AL-QAEDA: AN ASSESSMENT

In taking stock of Osama bin Laden and al-Qaeda, the pivotal question that must be answered is, "Were 9/11 and the subsequent events associated with it a victory or a defeat for al-Qaeda?" Bergen, an astute analyst of the al-Qaeda leader over the years, provides both a positive and negative answer to that question. In the first case, 9/11 thrust bin Laden and al-Qaeda before a global audience that witnessed in real time the most celebrated terrorist attack in modern history.

The 9/11 attacks were an enormous tactical success for al-Qaeda. They involved well-coordinated strikes on multiple targets in the heart of the enemy, magnified through their global broadcasts. The 9/11 'propaganda of the deed' took place in the media capital of the world, which ensured the 'widest possible coverage of the event' . . . al-Qaeda had been a largely unknown organization before 9/11, [but] in the days after it became a household name.[23]

73

Furthermore, 9/11 became a recruiting tool for al-Qaeda and other jihadist organizations, not to mention helping fill the depleted coffers of bin Laden's organization. Another plus for him was that the strike cost his organization only $500,000, while the United States was left with a bill of $500 billion.[24]

On the other side of the ledger, however, 9/11 was a strategic disaster for bin Laden and the Taliban. In the latter's case, the only jihadist-dominated country in the world — if one does not include Iran in that category — was crushed as a consequence of bin Laden's folly. In striking the United States, he failed to achieve his objective of dealing a deadly blow to the apostate Islamic regimes that were close to Washington. His "call did not resonate with the planet's more than one billion Muslims. Instead of mass outpourings of support for bin Laden, in the cities of Karachi and Jakarta there were demonstrations against the United States that only numbered in the low tens of thousands."[25] At the same time, Islamic governments rallied around the Americans in their anti-terrorist campaign and, perhaps of most significance, they did not expel Americans from Muslim lands but rather consolidated the U.S. military presence in many of them.

In conclusion, Bergen writes, "as the strategic leader of al-Qaeda, bin Laden has been an abject failure. His total dominance of al-Qaeda meant it was hostage to his strategic vision, and that became a problem for the organization because bin Laden's cult-like control over his group was not matched by any depth of strategic insight."[26]

Soon after the routing of the Taliban and al-Qaeda, a number of positive outcomes for the West materialized in Afghanistan:

- By the end of 2003, there was a dramatic decline in U.S. casualties; only 48 American military personnel were killed.
- Two million Afghans returned from exile, primarily from Pakistan and Iran.
- By 2005, most of the warlords were disarmed.
- Karzai proved to be an adept politician as he outmaneuvered his most potent competitors — people like the Uzbek General Dostum. In October 2004, he was elected president, and voter turnout was 70 percent — a result exceeding that of most similar elections in the United States.[27]

A PARTIAL VICTORY

Of course, Afghanistan had been beset for decades by wars that produced monstrous atrocities and material destruction. It was one of the world's poorest countries, where 7 out of 10 of its citizens were illiterate and knew little or nothing about the internet, e-mail, and other modern wonders that people in most corners of the world had taken for granted.

Consequently, the failure to provide significant development assistance guaranteed a gloomy future for Afghanistan.

> The 6,000 U.S. soldiers there in 2002 had one mission: to hunt the Taliban and al-Qaeda — not to secure the population or help in reconstruction, the classical tasks of a successful counterinsurgency campaign. In the words of the official U.S. military history of the Afghan War, 'the strong antipathy towards large-scale reconstruction and governance efforts at high levels in the US government persisted through 2002 and into 2003'.[28]

One might add that had the troops and resources devoted to the invasion of Iraq and its aftermath been deployed in Afghanistan, it is likely that the nation's "longest war" would have been successfully terminated years ago.[29] Arguably, the Taliban would have been dealt a lethal blow had the funds devoted to Iraq been spent on development and stabilization programs in Afghanistan.

ENDNOTES - CHAPTER 4

1. Richard A. Clarke, *Against All Enemies: Inside America's War on Terror,* New York: Free Press, 2004, p. 32.

2. Peter L. Bergen, *The Longest War,* New York: Free Press, 2011, p.52.

3. *Ibid.,* p. 54.

4. *Ibid.,* p. 52.

5. Alex Strick van Linschoten and Felix Kuehn, *Separating the Taliban from Al-Qaeda: The Core of Success in Afghanistan,* New York: Center on International Cooperation, February 2011, p. 5.

6. *Ibid.*

7. Bergen, p. 90.

8. *Ibid.,* p. 59.

9. *Ibid.,* p. 57.

10. While the Taliban remained a formidable enemy, Massoud was counting on help from tough allies such as Ismail Kahn who escaped from a Kandahar prison in February 2000. He also had the support of the brutal Uzbek General Dostum and, although suspicious of anti-Taliban leaders like Hamid Karzai, he was prepared to join them in dismantling the Pashtun Islamists who had expelled him from Kabul. Karzai had served as a Massoud depu-

ty in the Rabbanni government, but since he once supported the Taliban and lived in Pakistan under the watchful eye of the ISI, his loyalty was suspect. See Coll, who devotes significant space to Massoud's exploits.

11. Bob Woodward, *Bush at War*, New York: Simon & Schuster, 2002, p. 156.

12. Bergen, p. 91.

13. Stephen Biddle, *Afghanistan and the Future of Warfare: Implications for Army and Defense Policy*, Carlisle, PA: Strategic Studies Institute, U.S. Army War College, 2002, p. 14.

14. Van Linschoten and Kuehn, p. 8.

15. *Ibid.*, p. 4.

16. Bergen, pp. 73-74.

17. Woodward, p. 150. In 2010 in an election race against Abdullah Abdullah, a former foreign minister, Karzai was awarded the victory, although many observers in the country and abroad deemed the election bogus. After protesting it, Abdullah finally halted his campaign for another election. Karzai was the subject of much criticism in the American press, but he has complained that his side of the story has not been heard. He had good relations with the Bush administration, but it essentially ignored Afghanistan in its preoccupation with Iraq, while the Obama administration has compelled him to work with an Ambassador and special representative—Lieutenant General Karl Eikenberry and Richard Holbrooke—who, he charged, had showered him with unsubstantiated claims about his personal foibles and his official performance as president. Furthermore, Karzai has charged that the Americans have engaged in loose talk that not only humiliates him, but suggests that there are no Afghans who are capable of running their government.

18. Trita Parsai, *Treacherous Alliance*, New Haven, CT: Yale University Press, 2007, p. 228.

19. *Ibid*.

20. *Ibid.*

21. *Ibid.*

22. *Ibid.*, p. 229.

23. Bergen, p. 91.

24. *Ibid.*, p. 93.

25. *Ibid.*, pp. 175-176.

26. *Ibid.*, p. 94.

27. *Ibid.*, pp. 175-176.

28. *Ibid.*, p. 181.

29. For insight into the decisionmaking that led up to the Iraq War, see Steven Metz, *Operation IRAQI FREEDOM: Removing Saddam Hussein by Force*, Vol. 1, Carlisle, PA: Strategic Studies Instituite, U.S. Army War College, February 2010.

CHAPTER 5

THREE SCENARIOS

In anticipation of the 2011-14 "transition," U.S. planners must consider a range of plausible outcomes that will emerge at the end of that period. They will provide insight into a) the daunting challenges ahead, b) the prospects for new areas of cooperation with Russia in Afghanistan, and c) the conclusions and recommendations bearing on U.S. policy in the Greater Middle East.

THE EXISTING SITUATION OR PLAN A: AN UNSTABLE BUT VIABLE AFGHANISTAN THROUGH COIN

Early in 2009, after a 60-day assessment of U.S. operations in Afghanistan, President Barack Obama deployed 30,000 additional troops to the battlefield.[1] In a December 2010 report evaluating COIN operations in Afghanistan, the White House was cautiously optimistic about developments there. Progress had been made in reversing the Taliban's momentum; in denying them control of major communications and population centers; in disrupting their activities in the countryside; and in denying al-Qaeda sanctuaries in Afghanistan. In assessing what we have called Plan A, the situation was deemed hopeful, albeit "fragile." In subsequent statements by General Petraeus and Department of Defense (DoD) reports to Congress, much the same assessment was provided.[2]

Although a minority, some outside experts agreed with this prognosis. The National Defense University's Paul D. Miller noted that "the stabilization and reconstruction effort in Afghanistan has gone better than is widely believed." He reminded impatient critics that a coherent COIN plan was not in place until 2009, many years after the war began. "Although serious challenges remain, victory is attainable — if the troops and their civilian counterparts are given times to complete their mission."[3] Michael O'Hanlon of the Brookings Institution cited another reason for optimism: President Obama's decision to scrap the ill-conceived July 2011 exit point and to replace it with a 2014 deadline. This extension would give COIN more time to work. He also was heartened by a rise in Afghan security forces: "20,000 recruits are in training at all times, and the force is on pace to reach its interim goals of 134,000 soldiers by this fall." The ranks of the officer corps had undergone extensive training, with "these innovations having begun to yield results in combat, with increasingly positive reports of the performance of Afghan army formations against insurgents in the south and east of the country."[4] Likewise, real progress was being made in attacking the country's corrosive and widespread corruption.

In March 2011, General David Petraeus said, "The momentum of the Taliban has been halted in much of the country and reversed in some important areas."[5] In 2009 Kabul was surrounded by the insurgents, but in 2010 it was secure. Looking toward the spring, Petraeus focused on the interdiction of Taliban returning from sanctuaries in Pakistan, while negating jihadist efforts to regain control of territory that they lost as a consequence of the 2010 troop surge. Civilian casualties remained a point of friction with Karzai, but the general's relations with the Afghan President were cordial.

Generally, analysts outside of government were less confident about our chances in Afghanistan, with their darker appraisal resting upon the following observations.

The Insurgency.

According to the Center For American Progress, "The insurgency's ability to carry out operations does not appear to have been significantly weakened."[6] It has suffered losses in its leadership, but has the capacity to replace its fallen commanders. Simultaneously, in spite of considerable efforts to deny them funds, the militants continue to finance their efforts by dealing in drugs, stealing U.S. development money, imposing tariffs on commercial enterprises, and securing donations from wealthy Gulf State benefactors. It is plausible that some Taliban may be talking with Karzai because they are feeling the pressure, but others oppose reconciliation because they believe they are winning.

Other commentators claimed the insurgency is growing stronger, more widespread, more confident, and more sophisticated. It has suffered serious losses in skilled commanders, but it is unsettling that the people replacing them are younger, more militant, and infused with religious fervor.

The Karzai Government.

Official and expert opinions agree on one critical matter: the Karzai government is inefficient and has no national outreach. Even though it is autocratic, it cannot impose its will upon the provinces that are under the control of local business, religious leaders, and tribal elites, as well as criminal organizations and warlords. Then, of course, there is the shadow governments that the Taliban operate. Karzai lacks credibility with the people to no small degree because of widespread and pervasive corruption that he has not addressed. Worse yet, no one really believes that he will or can do so. He refuses to accept outside advice because of "his belief that we need him more than he needs us." He stubbornly adheres to this view even though more than 70 percent of his budget relies upon outside donors.[7]

Karzai is at odds with the new legislature that was elected in 2010, and there is growing evidence of ethnic discord in the country that reminds many of the violent friction that led to the post-Soviet civil war. Hazara, Tajik, and Uzbek leaders have chided Karzai for reneging on promises to give them more representation in the legislature and his cabinet. Since one of the basic principles of COIN is that it cannot work without good governance, it is difficult to be optimistic about developments in Afghanistan.

Security Forces.

Efforts to place more police personnel on the streets have been plagued by a number of setbacks: illiteracy, drug abuse, desertions, and conflicting loyalties. The shortfall of trainers has delayed turning raw recruits into functional law enforcement agents. Worse yet, when the police are deployed, the local population complains that they are corrupt, and allied commanders lament that they are reluctant to take on the insurgents, often turning the other way when the bad guys are in the neighborhood.

Reports pertaining to the Army are more upbeat. There is evidence that if properly equipped, led, and trained, it can take on the insurgents without allied help. It will be several years, however, before Afghan soldiers will have sufficient numbers to operate independently. Likewise, the drive to create a national Army has run up against local tribal chiefs who deem security their preserve. Those who are Pashtun are not pleased seeing heavily-armed Tajiks and Uzbeks strolling through their communities. However, though Tajiks are over-represented in the officer corps and the ranks of the noncommissioned officers (NCOs), they report to superiors who are largely Pashtuns.

Finally, in keeping with U.S. success in Iraq, the U.S. military is looking toward the creation of local paramilitary police units to deter the insurgents until regular Army units are prepared to do so. An American officer serving in Afghanistan reports, "They're supposed to be the neighborhood watch with AK-47s. But these guys are setting up checkpoints, they're doing classic militiaman shakedown things."[8]

The Civilian-Economic Component.

There must be an economic component to a successful COIN campaign, and on this score one can cite a number of positive developments in Afghanistan. Since 2002, economic and social programs have claimed 31 percent of U.S. expenditures in that country. As a consequence, there have been vast improvements, as S. Frederick Starr observed in January 2011:

> In public health, "90% of Afghan children under five have been vaccinated and 670 clinics opened."

> Hundreds of schools have been built and equipped with textbooks; more Afghan girls were enrolled in school than at any other time in the country's history.

Much progress has been made in constructing bridges and roads, and over time, efforts to sustain U.S. allied forces have provided a framework for the Northern Distribution Network.

And there is more: "Other projects in areas as varied as banking reform, small business development, financial services, land titling, business parks, credit support, and the reconstruction of markets have brought genuine economic gain."[9]

On June 8, 2011, however, the Majority Staff of the U.S. Senate Foreign Relations Committee released a report indicating that the civilian developmental component of the war in Afghanistan was seriously flawed. Funds were being provided without "robust oversight. Most U.S. aid bypasses the Afghan Government in favor of international firms." Salaries higher than the norm were being paid to workers who refused lesser paid government jobs and "unity of effort" on the part of the U.S. Government was missing.[10] Moreover, "high staff turnover, pressure from the military, imbalances between military and civilian resources, unpredictable funding levels from Congress, and changing political timelines have further complicated efforts. Pressure to achieve rapid results puts our civilians . . . under enormous strain to spend money quickly."[11] In sum, the report indicated that the primary goal of the program—"sustainability"—was not being met.

For many critics this is what they feared; that is, when all of the development programs were placed in perspective, what was being proposed was nothing less than nation-building. This prompted the disconcerting question: was the United States in a position to capitalize such a massive enterprise, given this country's own outsized economic difficulties? And would the American people continue to devote their tax dollars to a war that seemed to be unending?

Declining Support for the War within the United States.

The American electorate ignored the war in Afghanistan during the 2010 congressional elections, but when asked their opinions, voters were decidedly pessimistic. Early in 2011, a national sample of Americans opposed "the U.S. war in Afghanistan" by a 58 to 40 percent margin.

- 72 percent of the population favored a "speed up" in "the withdrawal of U.S. troops from Afghanistan.
- By a 51 to 41 percent margin, they said the United States "should not be involved in Afghanistan."
- Most Americans believed the war was "going badly."
- By a 46 to 45 percent margin, the American public said it "disapproved" of the way Obama was conducting the war.
- Finally, 60 percent said the war was "not worth fighting."[12]

Taken together, all of these observations support the view of many analysts that Plan A is not working, and its future prospects are slim. But its defenders contend that it can be a success if the following circumstances materialize:

- Pakistan resumes its campaign against the jihadists on its border with Afghanistan and denies them sanctuaries.

- The Afghan army demonstrates that it can fight without direct allied help. Of course, the thinned-out U.S. force will continue to provide air cover and extensive logistical support until 2014 and quite possibly for years beyond that point.
- The local police/militia ranks are swelling nationwide and demonstrating the resolve to confront the Taliban and their allies.
- The Karzai government has expanded its outreach to a cross section of society and has demonstrated a new resolve in combating corruption.
- As Taliban soldiers leave the battlefield in growing numbers, a significant portion of their leaders seek reconciliation with the government in Kabul.
- Should all of these events materialize, along with more positive economic metrics, public support for the government will dramatically improve.

Pakistan.

The Riedel Report underscored the important part that Pakistan will play in stabilizing Afghanistan. Today, the White House concedes that relations between Washington and Islamabad are problematic. Pakistani commentators, in turn, have specifically explained why this is the case, in the process assigning the lion's share of the blame to the United States:

- The jihadist violence that thrives in the region is a result of U.S. neglect on the one hand and inept policies on the other.

- In addition to helping spawn both al-Qaeda and the Taliban, U.S. missteps in Afghanistan have shredded Pakistan's social fabric and produced conditions that radical Islamists have exploited. Pakistan has suffered the awesome burden of caring for Afghan refugees running into the millions.
- By suspending assistance as punishment for Pakistan's nuclear program, Washington contributed to Islamabad's economic difficulties. Economic turmoil, in turn, has created conditions that extremists have exploited in the Federally Administered Tribal Areas (FATA).
- The United States has ignored the enormous contribution that Pakistan has made in confronting the common enemy. Since September 11, 2001 (9/11), Pakistan has devoted $35 billion to the fight and has suffered military casualties exceeding those suffered by allied units. At the same time, Pakistani civilians have been killed in the thousands.
- By conducting kill-and-capture operations and drone strikes against militants residing in Pakistan, the Americans have violated Islamabad's sovereignty. Indeed, the raid that killed bin Laden underscores Washington's contempt for Pakistani self-respect.
- The United States has failed to acknowledge Pakistan's specific concerns about Indian mischief in Afghanistan and New Delhi's refusal to reconcile differences over Kashmir, not to mention that India represents an actual military threat to its Islamic neighbor.
- Analysts in Islamabad are convinced that the Americans are plotting to create conditions

that ultimately result in the de-nuclearization of Pakistan.

- It is against this backdrop that 64 percent of the Pakistani population has identified the United States as "an enemy."[13]

This is not the place to engage in a comprehensive assessment of these charges; they will be addressed in our concluding remarks. But since the charges have been made public, U.S.-Pakistani relations have taken a turn for the worse, particularly since the Navy Seal raid upon bin Laden's compound located in the heart of a city filled with Pakistani military retirees and close to the country's nuclear facilities.

In conclusion, many critics of COIN do not believe that Plan A will succeed and that other options should be considered. One that has attracted some attention is a plan advocated by Robert Blackwill, the former U.S. Ambassador to India. It calls for partition of Afghanistan largely along ethnic lines.

PLAN B: PARTITION

According to Blackwill, "The Unites States and its allies are not on course to defeating the Taliban military." The combat units required are not in keeping with troop-to-population ratios. "Nor with an occupying army largely ignorant of local history, tribal structures, languages, customs, politics, and values, will the alliance win over large numbers of the Afghan Pashtuns, as counterinsurgency doctrine demands." What is more, Karzai's government is "corrupt" and will not "significantly improve," the Afghan army cannot "hold its own," and the public in the United States and "allied countries . . . is unlikely to permit the extension of the intervention for the length of time counterinsurgency doctrine says is required for success."[14]

In addition, Blackwill dwells upon the ethnic divisions in Afghan society, citing *The Economist*:

> Less than 3 percent of recruits are from the troublesome Pashtun south, from where the Taliban draw most support. Few will sign up, fearing ruthless intimidation against government 'collaborators' and their families. As a result, northern officers who only speak Dari have to use translators when in the Pashtu-speaking south. Northern infantry are reluctant to go there at all.[15]

Pivoting off the fractious ethnic situation, Blackwill has a solution to the Afghanistan Question: "de facto partition of the country." The administration should "stop talking about exit strategies and instead commit the United States to a long-term combat role in Afghanistan of 35,000-50,000 troops." In doing so, it must accept an unpleasant fact: "The Taliban will inevitably control most of the Pashtun south and east. . . ."[16]

In the western and northern sectors of Afghanistan, an entity comprised of the three dominant non-Pashtun ethnic communities, along with those Pashtuns who deem Taliban rule intolerable, will form their own sovereign political community — something along the lines of the Northern Alliance. They and their foreign supporters will keep the jihadists at bay through a counterterrorist strategy. Should the Taliban attack the anti-Taliban security zone, they will be met with devastating air attacks along with lethal mobile ground strikes from bases in the north. At the same time, it can be assumed that the Taliban will be preoc-

cupied with tribal opposition to its rule and guerrilla-
type resistance from other sources in Afghanistan's
east and south.

> In short, President Obama should announce that the
> United States and its Afghan and foreign partners will
> pursue a comprehensive counter-terrorism strategy in
> Pashtun Afghanistan and a nation-building strategy
> in the rest of the country, committing to both policies
> for at least the next 7 to 10 years. [17]

Blackwill's Plan B has attracted significant and
on occasion vitriolic criticism. Michael Rubin of the
American Enterprise Institute (AEI) calls it "ignorant, immoral, and dangerous."[18] It is ignorant because "Afghans" seldom lose wars, they just change
sides; it is immoral because it assumes "all Pashtun
must somehow favor the Taliban"; and it is dangerous among other things because, "The idea that the
Taliban would be satiated with just the Pashtun areas
is wrong-headed."[19]

Lieutenant General David Barno, the former U.S.
commander in Afghanistan, is equally critical of the
proposal because it ignores a trenchant fact: "Most Afghans want to remain a unified state of diverse ethnic
groups."[20] At the same time, Blackwill's plan would
prove to be devastating for Pakistan.

Khalid Aziz observes that:

> If Blackwill's policies are implemented, the existen-
> tialist threat to Pakistan will increase. The resulting
> chaos and violence may force the 40 million Pashtuns
> who reside in Pakistan to consider the dynamics of
> establishing a separate state. Given Pakistan's ethnic
> fragility and simmering discontent in Baluchistan,
> Blackwill's prescription will destabilize Pakistan.[21]

In spite of Plan B's flaws, U.S. planners must look at Blackwill's proposal in all seriousness. Among other things, partition may occur despite U.S. intentions as a consequence of events on the ground, such as the eventual unraveling of Plan A or some other catalyst to civil war.

Afghanistan may have functioned as a single nation for centuries but the Soviet invasion, the civil war that followed it, Taliban rule, a largely foreign-led campaign to crush the Taliban, and a similar effort to deny their return to power have exacerbated ethnic enmity. In conflict associated with the 2010 parliamentary elections and efforts to create a cabinet in the Karzai government, ethnicity was a central point of discord. General Dostum, Chief of Staff to the Commander in Chief, His Excellency President Hamid Karzai — as well as the head of Uzbek-dominated Junbesh-e Milli party — has accused Karzai of "ethnic favoritism" in his interpretation of the hotly disputed election outcome. Likewise, Hazara politicians associated with the mainly Hazara Hesb-e-Wahdat Party have chastised Karzai for reneging on promises to appoint their people to cabinet positions.[22]

Observers of President Karzai's personnel reshuffling in the Ministry of Defense and ANA have observed that it has "occurred in the context of increasing ethnic factionalism, both in the ANA and in Afghan politics in general."[23] The case of Amrullah Saleh, a Tajik who was Minister of the National Directorate of Security (NDS) — and a close associate of Massoud — is cited as an example of Karzai seeking to marginalize non-Pashtun leaders. He was fired by Karzai, but foreign observers think highly of him and his name comes to mind when one considers who might be one of the leaders to rule a rump state in the north, were partition to become a reality. Another name that surfaces is Abdullah Abdullah, the former close associate of Massoud who almost defeated Karzai in the last race for the presidency.

In considering the case for partition, the following observations deserve close attention:

- There is ample evidence that ethnic discord may have reached the point where the centrifugal forces of fragmentation exceed those that promote national unity. Developments in Iraq have taken much the same course. As Ayad Allawi, the former secular Shiite prime minister of Iraq has indicated, decades of sectarian violence in Iraq have fostered similar toxic relations among ethnic communities there.[24]

- By reducing the field of battle and excluding a population that harbors their Pashtun rivals, military operations for a reduced Afghanistan become more manageable.

- In response to Pakistan's opposition to partition, two compelling observations are in order. First, short of a government under its thumb, there are few options that promote stability in Afghanistan that are acceptable to Pakistan. Second, the prospect of partition may serve as an incentive for Islamabad to deny the jihadists a safe harbor in Pakistan and to help resolve the Afghanistan Question. In this connection, the notion that the Pashtuns on both sides of the Durand Line might join forces in an attempt to create an independent Pashtun state is one of Islamabad's most chilling nightmares.

- As the U.S. 2012 presidential election approaches, it will be difficult for any candidate to claim that America's longest war is cost effective, and options once considered unthinkable may become plausible.

- Finally, to avoid even bloodier fighting and countless atrocities, many Afghans may prefer partition—if endorsed by the international community—to civil war or Taliban rule. Clearly, there is more than sufficient cause for U.S. defense planners to consider partition as plausible and deserving of close scrutiny.

A TALIBAN VICTORY

U.S. planners must contemplate Plan C, the unthinkable: the Taliban return to power. It, however, could take one of two paths.

The Global Jihadists Prevail.

The first involves the emergence of jihadists who cling to bin Laden's dream of creating a 21st century Islamic Caliphate that dominates most of the Islamic world. Under these circumstances, we can anticipate the resumption of the following harsh policies that the Taliban championed during their brief rule from 1996 until 2001:

- The imposition of Sharia law upon the 30 million people living in Afghanistan that previously resulted in international condemnation of wholesale human rights violations.
- Diplomatic recognition by Pakistan and Saudi Arabia and perhaps several other Islamic-dominated countries as least in initial stages of resuming power.
- A campaign to export their brand of jihad into Central Asia and Russia proper.
- Terrorist strikes against the United States.

As long as U.S. forces are in Afghanistan, this outcome will not materialize. In response to overt attacks, there is no question that the United States would take appropriate military action, but the deployment of general purpose forces would not be required; counterterrorist strikes along with punishing attacks upon the Taliban's infrastructure could do the job.

But given the Taliban's experience in 2001, it is inconceivable that the new generation of leaders would support overt attacks of this kind. How could they possibly forget the devastating 2001 U.S. response to 9/11? There are many Taliban observers who contend that they have learned their lesson: they realize that, if they once again followed the advice of their most fanatical jihadist allies, they would be committing suicide.

After all, trends were moving in their favor by 2001: Massoud could not have survived much longer, and with him gone, the Taliban would have had the entire country under their control. Thus Ahmed Rashid believes that if they return to power, the Taliban will not provoke the Americans once again by providing al-Qaeda with refuge or adopt their own fanatical anti-American terrorist agenda. Many American commentators are of the same opinion, arguing as well that most insurgents in Afghanistan are ethnic Pashtuns "who are focused on a local agenda and do not have global aspirations or the means to act outside their immediate area."[25]

The Taliban Return to Power with a National Agenda.

Many Taliban were outraged by bin Laden's provoking the Americans into a crushing retaliatory blow against Afghanistan. Those who currently think in similar terms are likely to abide by the advice of Pakistani and Saudi supporters that should they return to power, they must avoid provocative anti-Western terrorist acts. The same would hold true for the jihadists that might live among them.

Then, too, as they seek to redevelop their country after decades of war, it will be prudent for pragmatists among them to engage and not confront their neighbors — such as those in Central Asia, China, India, Iran, Pakistan, and Russia. Many commentators overlook that in the last years of the Taliban rule before 9/11, the government and society that it dominated were on the cusp of collapse. Why should anyone believe, then, that a revitalized Taliban regime has any hope of becoming a more viable entity today than it did yesterday? The only way that could happen would be with massive outside assistance.

Likewise, the Taliban would have to adjust to significant changes in the international strategic environment where peaceful roads to regime change, and not violence, have succeeded. The younger and democratic middle class elements associated with the Arab Spring exist in other Islamic communities; for them, the jihadists represent all that is reactionary and brutal, and thus are an unacceptable model for society. The jihadists then will find that their roadmap for reform is welcomed only in countries that are in the most advanced stages of economic and political disintegration, such as Yemen and Somalia.

One more observation must be underscored in considering "worst case" scenarios pertaining to Afghanistan. Recall that many U.S. defense commentators supported the Vietnam War in no small part because it was widely believed that a communist victory there would spread the communist contagion throughout the Far East. That did not happen. Indeed, in the summer of 1979, the communist Chinese government and its counterparts in Hanoi fought a brief but bloody war along their common border. What is more, our failure in Vietnam can be seen as the failure of Washington to understand that nationalism, not Marxism, explained why the Vietnamese peasants were fighting with such valor against the latest Western imperial force that had invaded their country. Perhaps just as our exaggerated fear of communism hampered our critical faculties during the Cold War, like-minded fears about Islamic terrorism are distorting our strategic vision today. For example, consider the absurd claim that our society is in danger of being subverted by Sharia law.

That said, the most radical and violent jihadists do not need Afghanistan or Pakistan to launch terrorists attacks against the West and moderate Islamic countries; they can plot their evil deeds in Yemen, Somalia, North Africa, and South East Asia, not to mention Hamburg, London, or New York. Moreover, the Arab Spring may ultimately create conditions that the jihadists will exploit to their advantage. But note that in each of these cases, the proper response to them is not COIN but a more limited counterterrorist campaign. After all, terrorist experts in the West have indicated that the most recent strikes against U.S. and allied targets have been conducted by lone wolves. This is not to ignore terrorist strikes capable of producing significant casualties or physical destruction. To burnish his image, Zawahiri, the new al-Qaeda leader, would relish a success of this kind but trends appear to support those who see more limited attacks as the most likely to materialize in the years ahead. We must be vigilant but not exaggerate the capacities of the jihadists.

ENDNOTES - CHAPTER 5

1. For a comprehensive discussion of the Riedel Report, see Bob Woodward, *Obama's Wars*, New York: Simon and Schuster, 2010, pp. 99-110.

2. The White House, *Report in Afghanistan and Pakistan*, Washington, DC: Executive Office of the President, 2010.

3. Paul Miller, "Finish the Job," *Foreign Affairs*, January-February 2011, pp. 51-52.

4. Michael O' Hanlon, "Staying Power: The U.S. Mission in Afghanistan beyond 2011," *Foreign Affairs*, September-October, 2010, p. 71.

5. Carlotta Gall, "Petraeus Sees Military Progress in Afghanistan," *New York Times*, March 8, 2011.

6. Caroline Wadhams *et al.*, "Realignment: Managing a Stable Transition to Afghan Responsibility," *Americanprogress.org*, November 2010, p. 8.

7. Update Briefing, "Afghanistan's Elections Stalemate," Washington, DC: International Crisis Group, February 23, 2011, p. 1. "The prolonged crisis over Afghanistan's parliamentary elections has further undermined President Hamid Karzai's credibility. He is now even more isolated politically than he was after his dubious re-election in 2009."

8. Joshua Partlow, "U.S. effort to arm Afghan villagers carries some risk," *Washington Post*, February 7, 2011.

9. S. Frederick Starr, "Afghanistan Beyond the Fog of Nation Building: Giving Economic Strategy a Chance," Central Asia-Caucasus Institute Silk Road Studies Program, January 2011, pp. 6-12. Starr went on to claim, however, that the existing economic development program for Afghanistan is insufficient because it focuses only on agricultural development and exploitation of natural resources. They must be supplemented with the "Silk Road strategy" that involves restoration of a commercial transit route that existed in antiquity and would serve the economic interests

of the Central Asian countries and China, India, Iran, and Pakistan. In passing, he notes that "the reopening of all these age-old transit routes across Afghanistan is the single greatest achievement of U.S. foreign policy in the new millennium." *Ibid.*, p. 13.

10. "Evaluating U.S. Foreign Assistance To Afghanistan," *A Majority Staff Report*, Washington, DC: Committee on Foreign Relations United States Senate, June 8, 2011, pp. 3-4.

11. *Ibid.*, pp. 13-14.

12. *PollingReport.com*, January 2011, pp. 1-5. After bin Laden was killed, support for the war took an upswing, as did Obama's conduct of the conflict in the eyes of the American people, but the major negative trend lines persisted.

13. Malik Zafar Iqbal, "An Appraisal of the Afghanistan-Pakistan Strategy to Counter Terrorism," *Parameters*, Summer 2010, p. 17.

14. Robert D. Blackwill, "Plan B in Afghanistan," *Foreign Affairs*, January/February 2011, pp. 42-43.

15. *Ibid.*, p. 43.

16. *Ibid.*, p. 44.

17. *Ibid.*

18. Michael Rubin, "A Very Bad Plan For Afghanistan," *The National Review Online*, September 15, 2010, p. 1.

19. *Ibid.*

20. Thomas E. Ricks, "Bob Blackwill's bad bad Afghan Plan B: Let's surrender but then keep fighting!" *FinancialTimes.com*, January 6, 2011.

21. Khalid Aziz, "A plan for Afghanistan's partition," *The Express Tribune*, November 9, 2010. Also see NATO's General Secretary Anders Fogh Rasmussen's critical comments in *Pakistan Patriot*, "Robert Blackwill's 'Plan B' is perpetual mimetic war in Afghanistan," September 16, 2010.

22. Pamela Brown, "Analysis Of The Afghan Defense Appointments," *Backgrounder*, Institute for the Study of War, July 20, 2010.

23. *Ibid.*, p. 1.

24. Anthony Shadid, "Iraq's Last Patriot," *New York Times Magazine*, February 6, 2011, p. 43.

25. Alex Strick van Linschoten and Felix Kuehn, *Separating the Taliban from Al-Qaeda: The Core of Success in Afghanistan*, New York: Center on International Cooperation, February 2011, p. 5.

CHAPTER 6

THE RUSSIAN RESPONSE

After the September 11, 2001 (9/11) al-Qaeda attacks, Russian president Putin was one of the first world leaders to offer Bush his condolences. The Islamic jihadists provided the two with a common foe and an opening for improving relations between their two countries. But that would not happen as Putin joined Bush's French and German allies in opposing the U.S. invasion of Iraq.

The Americans and Russians signed the 2002 Moscow Treaty reducing nuclear weapons but by the end of Bush's second term, Putin had concluded that fruitful discussions with him over a range of issues was a nonstarter. Moscow reacted favorably to Obama's election to no small degree because he indicated that he welcomed warmer relations with Russia and assumed that a John McCain victory would not unfreeze American-Russian relations.

In the spring of 2009, Obama met with Russian President Dmitry Medvedev in Europe, and later with Prime Minister Putin, indicating that he favored a reset in relations with Russia. In the 2010 *U.S. National Security Strategy* statement, Obama said, "We seek to build a stable, substantive, multidimensional relationship with Russia, based on mutual interests."[1]

Skeptics in the United States discredited the policy, but it was in keeping with one favored by Republican statesmen like Henry Kissinger and George Shultz who argued that harmonious relations with Russia were vital to U.S. security objectives—fighting global terrorism, stemming the proliferation of nuclear weapons, and addressing global warming.[2]

The most immediate opportunity for a reset in relations was the ratification of the New Strategic Arms Reduction Treaty (START) that Obama and Medvedev endorsed in their spring meeting. From that time forward, they would begin the reset campaign in earnest. In November 2010, at the NATO Summit in Lisbon, Portugal, Medvedev reaffirmed and expanded upon Russia's assistance to coalition operations in Afghanistan. Obama, in turn, promised to give Moscow a voice in a new European missile defense system that replaced the proposal in Eastern Europe that Bush had favored but which some in the Kremlin deemed a threat to their nuclear strike force.

Then in 2010, the reset was given a boost from an unexpected quarter: a warming in relations between Poland and Russia appeared after a tragic plane crash in Russia. It resulted in the death of the Polish President, Lech Kaczynski, and many prominent Polish civilian and military leaders. Zbigniew Brzezinski, a man whose name does not bring smiles to the faces of the Kremlin overlords, characterized Putin's expression of solace as genuine. "I do not think that this is a game on the part of Russia," he wrote in *Time Magazine*, "this is something sincere and very new." If it endured, "it will be geo-politically . . . equal to the importance of German-Polish reconciliation."[3]

Despite a subsequent dispute over who was responsible for the accident, the Poles eventually conceded that their pilot had ignored the advice of Russian air-traffic controllers and landed in fog-shrouded Smolensk. It was alleged that the Polish president compelled him to land the aircraft in spite of the awful weather conditions.

But to place the American-Russian reset in proper perspective, a closer look at the Russian response to 9/11 is in order. Soon after the attacks, the State Department's Richard Armitage and the CIA's Cofer Black flew to Moscow to brief the Russians and to forewarn them that a U.S. military strike against the Taliban was in the works. The response was positive, and a Russian team was sent to Washington to share information about the major features of Afghanistan's topography and other ground intelligence that they had gathered in the 1980s. The American infiltration teams relied upon Russian maps to help them navigate Afghanistan's difficult terrain and to identify areas that should be avoided by the invading forces. It also provided cold weather equipment and other gear to protect the Americans against the harsh conditions they would encounter.

Moscow encouraged the Northern Alliance to provide an infantry complement to assist the American special operation forces and the small U.S. contingent of regular soldiers that would confront the Taliban and their al-Qaeda allies.[4] The Alliance had officers and men who knew the area well and had engaged the Taliban in deadly firefights over many years.

Putin said in a telephone conversation with Bush, "We are going to support you in the war on terror." But "we can't put any Russian troops on the ground in Afghanistan." That would have served neither Washington's nor Moscow's interest as it would provide the Taliban with a powerful propaganda coup. But Russia would provide the Northern Alliance troops with arms and ammunition — assistance that Moscow had made available to Massoud and his men for years. On the diplomatic front, Putin agreed to intervene with the Central Asian leaders and encouraged them to give the Americans access to their territory as long as the U.S. war on terror was "temporary and . . . not permanent."[5]

Putin's offer to help in combat search and air rescue (CSAR) operations was especially welcomed. It was standard operating procedure for the Pentagon to have CSAR capabilities in place when U.S. aircraft were at risk, and President Bush was acutely aware of the distasteful prospect of the Taliban exploiting captured American personnel for propaganda value. Both Jimmy Carter and Ronald Reagan could testify to the wisdom of that concern.

Diplomatically, Russia supported the Bush administration on a number of fronts. With its permanent seat in the UN Security Council, Russia provided the United States the legal justification for military action against the Taliban in Afghanistan. Then it supported the Bonn agreement and the selection of a pro-American Afghan as the country's new leader. Moscow would provide additional diplomatic help, although at times reluctantly.[6]

While Russia did not provide troops in Afghanistan, it did play an important role in meeting the coalition's logistical requirements. For example, from the very outset of the war, the International Security Assistance Force (ISAF) would rely upon the heavy air transport capability of Russia and Ukraine. Western payments for this service provided badly needed revenue, underscoring the economic advantages of cooperating with the West that even hardline opponents to the reset could not ignore.

Nonetheless, Russian commanders were wary of U.S. intentions and opposed Putin's offers of help. They were concerned in particular about Washington requesting and receiving assistance from the Uzbek and Tajik governments, specifically the use of air bases and land corridors to help facilitate the insertion of U.S. special forces and regular troops into Northern

Afghanistan. After all, the Kremlin leadership persisted in its claim that the "Five Stans" were located in Moscow's "sphere of special influence." Some in the security services pressured their old Central Asian comrades to reject American bids for basing rights and sought ways to break agreements that were already in force.

But while Moscow had the capacity to lean on the Central Asian leaders, several of them saw benefits in cooperation with the Americans. The U.S. Government found that Tajikistan was favorable to any request for access to its territory. Planners in Washington sought a land corridor from there to Northern Afghanistan rather than rely upon airlifts alone. It would facilitate the delivery of humanitarian as well as military cargo. It was through Tajikistan that CIA teams were inserted into Afghanistan to join the Northern Alliance forces and with the help of regular Army units eventually defeat the jihadists.

The Uzbek President Islam Karimov proved to be more resistant to complying with Washington's requests for assistance. He allowed the CIA to fly *Predator* drones from his territory, but in return he asked for generous economic aid, a mutual defense treaty, and even NATO membership. Such bold demands raised eyebrows in Moscow and did not sit well with NATO members who were wary of "out of area" commitments and intimate ties with dictators. He did provide an airfield even though it had limited capacity to handle heavy cargo planes like the C-5.[7]

In taking stock of Russia's support for the U.S.-led military victory over the Taliban and al-Qaeda, it is apparent that Moscow's help was critical. Without it, the United States would have had difficulty securing staging areas and corridors in Central Asia that facilitated an invasion from the North. Russia's flow of arms to the Northern Alliance was vital as well. Though we must not exaggerate Russia's cooperation, critics of joint American-Russian security ventures have been remiss in failing to acknowledge its assistance in the earliest phase of America's longest war.

But what about today and the reappearance of the Taliban? Some observers have characterized Russian help as "paltry," but that assessment may be too churlish. For example, Russia continues to provide intelligence germane to the success of coalition forces in Afghanistan; its security services, civilian and military, have considerable outreach throughout Central Asia as well as within Afghanistan, and their ability to help will surely grow.

The Russians have provided the Afghan security forces with small arms and other military equipment—albeit for a price. The Afghans are familiar with Russian small arms like the Kalashnikovs, and seem to prefer this assault weapon over American alternatives. Most recently, Russia has sold the Afghans 21 helicopters that are well-suited for both the harsh mountainous and dry desert conditions that prevail throughout the country. This sale had been facilitated through a Russia-NATO Council special program making it possible to finance "helicopter packages" that not only include the Mi-17 helicopters, but spare parts, maintenance, and training.[8] The copters will not be provided free of charge, but Moscow will defer some of the cost.

Many Afghan pilots are in their mid-40s or older, having learned to fly during the Soviet period, while others—mechanics and associated ground personnel—are familiar with Russian aircraft. As U.S. forces thin out and Afghan troops grow in number, an increasing percentage of them will be provided with

Russian arms and training. Some are already attending schools in Russia.

In judging Russia's role as security partner in Afghanistan, there are three case studies that can help us determine how effective that help has been and may be in the future. On the whole, the picture is positive but mixed.

COUNTERING AFGHAN NARCOTICS

Public opinion polls consistently show that when asked why they should be concerned about Afghanistan, Russians by an overwhelming margin specify drugs, not terrorism. There is ample reason why this is the case. "In Russia an estimated 30,000 to 40,000 people die of drug overdoses yearly. This amounts to more than the total number of soldiers killed during the entire Soviet campaign in Afghanistan between 1979 and 1989."[9] Most of the heroin, for example, that poisons Russian addicts comes from Afghan fields and drug labs.

At the same time, the importation and sale of drugs are facilitated by criminal organizations that exploit the corruption that prevails in Russia and its former Soviet republics. Those criminal organizations in turn are frequently tied to terrorists groups for financial, not ideological, reasons, but nonetheless their joint ventures help facilitate the arming of terrorists worldwide. It is with this knowledge in mind that Western observers rightly point out that corruption in Russia is a major reason why addicts there are dying in such large numbers.[10]

But even when conceding their own complicity, Russian analysts complain that their Western partners have failed to curtail the harvesting of poppies in Afghanistan. In 2005, the NATO-Russian Council (NRC) created the "NRC Project on Counter-Narcotics Training of Afghan and Central Asian Personnel," and Washington claims that it and other efforts have curtailed the production of poppies. Officials in Moscow disagree with this positive assessment of the ISAF's response to the drug crisis, asserting that since 2001 poppy production has increased. Moreover, the Russian Ambassador to the NRC, Dmitry Rogozin, has noted that the United States has been successful in eradicating drugs in Colombia, in part because the ratio of soldiers to hectares is far more favorable there than in Afghanistan. Why? Well the narcotics in Colombia are destined for the United States, while in Afghanistan, they are sold in Russia.[11]

Russian officials have an additional explanation for the American's reluctance to eliminate the drug trade: they do not want to risk casualties associated with drug interdiction, nor to anger Karzai, whose late brother Wali was fingered as a drug lord in the city of Kandahar. It is with such observations in mind that many Kremlin opponents of cooperation with the Americans deem it a bad deal for Russia. It is just the latest example of an American president getting concessions from Russia, while he delivers nothing but rhetoric in return.

Meanwhile, those in the United States who have a dim view of reset cite Moscow's duplicitous posture on the U.S. transit base in Manas, Kyrgyzstan, to support their case.

THE STRUGGLE OVER MANAS

The Manas Air Transit Center is located near Kyrgyzstan's capital of Bishkek. It has been a major transit point for ISAF and U.S. personnel and equipment going to and from Afghanistan ever since it was established in December 2001. From there, coalition planes have provided close air support, the shipment of cargo, and refueling missions.

Moscow viewed an American base at Manas with considerable anxiety, but the government in Bishkek welcomed the handsome rent that Washington offered for its use. In 2005, the Russian and Chinese governments sought to have it closed, expressing concern that its real function was to compromise their security. In Russia's case, the Tulip Revolution of March 2005 that deposed the Soviet-era Kyrgyz dictator, Askar Akayev, was interpreted as part of the Bush administration's campaign of "regime change" throughout the former USSR.

Although the Sino-Russian drive to oust the Americans failed, 4 years later after a rent-hike dispute, there was a second attempt to do so. That did not happen because in June Washington agreed to pay $60 million annually for the airfield. This action was preceded by an announced deal between Russia and Kyrgyzstan whereby the latter would receive a $2 billion loan from Moscow conditional upon the Americans' expulsion from Manas. Even though that ploy failed, Secretary Gates complained that Moscow was trying to have it "both ways; simultaneously working with and against the U.S. in the fight against the jihadists in Afghanistan."[12]

The Kremlin tried to make mischief for the Americans elsewhere in Central Asia. In 2005, when Washington chastised Uzbekistan's President Karimov for human rights abuses, officials in the Kremlin encouraged him to expel the United States from an airbase in his country and were successful. Moscow sought to compromise U.S. cooperation with Tajikistan by claiming the Americans were plotting to depose its President Emomali Rakmonov. This accusation was revealed by Tajikistan's Ambassador to the United States, Homraphon Zaripove, in a conversation with the American Ambassador to his country, Richard E. Hoagland. Under pressure from Moscow, Tajikistan's pro-Russian Ministry of Security contended "that the United States wants to overthrow Rakmonov, kick the Russians out of their military base, and expand U.S. influence from Afghanistan into Tajikistan as a link to 'U.S.-dominated Kyrgyzstan.' The U.S. goal in this scenario is a 'string of anti-Russia military bases from Baghram to Manas'."[13]

American opponents of a reset with Russia cite behavior of this nature to support their claim that anyone who believes that the Kremlin is serious about security cooperation is living in a fantasy land. The old guard in Russia's military community, they note, condones security cooperation with the West only if it serves Moscow's purposes.

THE NORTHERN DISTRIBUTION NETWORK

Whereas Russian critics of the reset cite the failure of the American-led coalition to curb the Afghan drug trade, and their U.S. counterparts complain about Manas, supporters in both countries cite the success of the Northern Distribution Network (NDN) as evidence that security cooperation can work.

It is a commonplace of military planning that logistics is a key to victory. Providing for the needs of coalition forces in the Afghan theater is a truly essential, but daunting, enterprise. The distances involved are long, and the routes are difficult and dangerous. Most of the equipment and supplies required by allied forces transit from the port of Karachi through the Khyber Pass and then to bases in Afghanistan. Over the years, many trucks have been destroyed during this transit, and American as well as Afghan and Pakistani personnel have been killed. Secretary of the Navy Ray Mabus has observed, "A lot of these convoys are hit with improvised explosive devices or with ambushes, sometimes before they even get to Afghanistan. For every 24 convoys, we lose an American killed or wounded. That is too high of a price to pay for energy."[14] Furthermore, the government of Pakistan on occasion has halted the flow of material to underline its unhappiness with American drone attacks within Pakistan or the infiltration of small units to kill or capture Taliban and al-Qaeda commanders seeking a safe harbor there. Still, as late as the spring of 2010, about 70 percent of the ammunition, food, gasoline, water, and other supplies moved through this route. This problematic situation provided an incentive for Washington to consider another way to provide for the troops in Afghanistan; a second route emerged after President Obama endorsed a surge in U.S. troops that would raise the number to close to 100,000 by the end of 2010.

Logistical experts point out that the difficulties encountered in shipping cargo to Afghanistan are monumental. In addition to the huge volume of cargo, there are many other problems.

> Because Afghanistan offers little in the way of basic infrastructure, the military has to build things like housing. That means that in addition to moving people and their equipment into the country, it also has to bring in construction materials, food, medicine, and munitions, along with support contractors and everything else needed to survive in one of the most diffi-

cult environments on earth. Then there's the challenge of finding a way to bring all that stuff into the country. Afghanistan has only 16 airports with paved runways, and only four are capable of handling international cargo traffic. There are no seaports—it is a landlocked nation. And there are no railroads in.[15]

Under these circumstances, "the U.S. military has been forced to rely mainly on roads to bring supplies into Afghanistan. But the situation there is not much better. Because the United States is barred from moving goods through Iran, points of entry into Afghanistan by ground are limited to a handful of mountain passes."[16] But the Khyber Pass and the crossing point through the Hindu Kush at Spin Boldak have been interdicted on numerous occasions by the insurgents. For example, "in December 2008, 12 percent of the Afghan-bound freight crossing Pakistan's Northwest Frontier Province en route to the Khyber Pass disappeared, most of it in flames."[17]

The NDN was established in February 2009 to provide coalition forces with an alternative to the perilous Pakistan corridors. It was initially comprised of two pathways: one in the north that begins at the Baltic Sea ports of Latvia—and more recently Klaipeda, Lithuania, as well—through Ukraine, Russia, and Kazakhstan to Afghanistan. "The southern section, known as NDN South, starts at the Georgian port of Poti. Cargo there is placed on rail cars that travel through Georgia and Azerbaijan, then across the Caspian Sea by boat into the port of Aktau in Kazakhstan. From there, the loads are trucked through Uzbekistan."[18] These two NDN corridors provide nonlethal supplies "amounting to 40 percent of what the coalition requires. As of the end of March 2010, over 10,000 containers had moved through the new set of routes."[19]

It is apparent that the NDN will expand operations as a result of a logistics hub that Korean Air has established at Uzbekistan's Navoi Airport. Cargo service associated with Korean Air carries loads to Delhi and Mumbai, India; Bangkok, Thailand; and Frankfurt, Germany. New routes to Dubai, United Arab Emirates (UAE); Almaty, Kazakhstan; and Dhaka, Bangladesh, will be included by the end of 2011. Supplies today are also making their way by rail from Siberia.

In addition to Moscow's cooperation, several Central Asian states have contributed to the logistical campaign as well. Unfortunately, on occasion the flow of material through the NDN has been disrupted as a result of bottlenecks in Tajikistan and Uzbekistan, and as a consequence of disputes between these two countries over the movement of rail carriages. The flow of supplies through the airspace, highways, and railroads has become especially crucial. They are not in the best of shape, and, what is more, U.S. observers note that the human rights practices of President Karimov leave much to be desired despite unofficial U.S. efforts at the person-to-person level to promote Uzbekistan liberalization.

In the late fall of 2010, the United States and NATO expanded the NDN through two agreements with Russia and another one with Kazakhstan. First, Moscow allowed a revision in the category of cargo that could be delivered via NDN such as armored vehicles — not tanks, but armored personnel carriers. A second agreement permitted the ISAF to move cargo from Afghanistan back to Europe. (The cargo costs of land shipment was 90 percent lower than air.) Third, Kazakhstan gave a green light for U.S. planes to fly over the North Pole and cross its territory into Afghanistan.[20] Finally, on February 25, 2011, when the

Russian Duma endorsed the new provisions, commentators anticipated that the Kremlin would soon allow lethal material to be included in the NDN shipments. There appears to be some uncertainty, however, about the status of all of these latest agreements. Nonetheless, in assessing the NDN, it is indisputable that it has made a significant contribution to the West's military campaign in Afghanistan.[21]

In addition to these new initiatives, Russia continues to be the source for most of the massive supply of gas and jet fuel that are required by the coalition's ground and air units.

CENTRAL ASIA AND THE NORTH CAUCASUS

Some final words on Russia and the three scenarios will be provided in the concluding chapter. Here the reasons why Moscow has compelling incentives to cooperate with the United States in the struggle against the jihadists will be underscored. Even if its contribution is modest, it will remain important as Washington's NATO allies are finding it ever more difficult to secure popular support for the struggle. Moreover, plans to draw down NATO are already in place; for example, the Europeans will be returning home before the 2014 time frame approaches. Russia, then, may be able to pick up some of the slack that materializes — although, it will not perform combat operations.

Central Asia is of major strategic importance to Russia for a number of pivotal reasons. The two most important are: first, that its hydrocarbon wealth and system of pipelines are critical to the success of Putin's "2020" modernization campaign; second, that if jihadists gain control of the five former Soviet Central Asian Republics, Russia would face a serious jihadist threat on its southern borders.[22]

With the collapse of the Soviet Union, the Central Asian countries cut lose from Moscow, but as a result they lost billions of rubles in subsidies, they lost millions of talented Russians who returned home, dictators came to rule with an iron fist, and, in a maelstrom of ethnic discord and economic decline, the Islamists found much to celebrate. Jihadist movements appeared both in Uzbekistan and Tajikistan and launched armed operations against the home-grown dictators and/or helped the Taliban and al-Qaeda gain power in Afghanistan. As Ahmed Rashid found in his conversations with Tajiks and Uzbeks and other Islamic radicals in the region during the Soviet war, they were "convinced that an Afghan victory would lead to Islamic revolutions throughout Central Asia."[23] They belonged to various radical sects of Sunni Islam; whereas Jihad previously had been associated with Iranian Shiites, now Sunnis had grasped the sword. Although the Soviet anti-religion campaign helped attenuate the influence of Islam in the Central Asian republics, the Muslim faithful went underground much as Christians did in the Baltic states. As noted earlier, the Soviet leadership during the Afghan War was stunned when it received reports that soldiers from Central Asia expressed pro-mujahedeen sentiments and watched with admiration as the jihadists courageously fought units of the Red Army. Some refused to engage their "brothers" on the battlefield and, in some instances, joined them. Indeed, many Muslims in the USSR were introduced into the wider world of Islam by serving in Afghanistan or by closely tracking news from the war zone.

Like many of the Afghan Islamists, they were exposed to more sophisticated mentors of global jihad in the cities of Pakistan and in the camps in the country's tribal zones. Under the tutelage of the "Arabs," they learned how to wage war against better armed adversaries and to win the support of ordinary folk that protected them and alerted them to the enemy's movements.

Many analysts believe that Central Asia is tottering on the abyss of chaos as the region's governments have proven incapable of stabilizing their societies. At the same time, they all face huge economic and social problems. By any measure, the situation in the region will deteriorate further should the Americans fail in Afghanistan. (At least this appears to be the assumption of Russian analysts.) Jihadists, local and foreign, have been active throughout the region for years, and the stark truth is that the coalition's failure in Afghanistan would represent a far greater threat to Russia and Central Asia than to the United States and Europe. Even critics of the reset in Moscow have acknowledged this truism.

Strategically, the Fergana Valley is the most valued territory since it knits together Uzbekistan, Kyrgyzstan, and Tajikistan and is home to about half of their collective populations. Should the Taliban regain power in Afghanistan, they are likely to promote insurgencies throughout the valley and compromise the security of pro-Russian and secular governments there. Needless to say, the resulting mayhem will menace those Russian business enterprises that are linked with the development and shipment of the region's hydrocarbon wealth. It is prudent, therefore, for Russia to provide whatever assistance that it can muster to promote an outcome in Afghanistan that does not place Central Asia at risk.

Arguably, the most aggressive Central Asia jihadist group is the Islamic Movement of Uzbekistan

(IMU), which grew in effectiveness while licking its wounds in its sanctuary in Pakistan's Waziristan region. The Islamic Movement of Uzbekistan jihadists suffered grievously in the face of the 2001 allied assaults, but they regrouped in Pakistan and have returned to Central Asia with a new élan, even though one of their founders, Tahir Yuldash, was killed in a U.S. drone attack in South Waziristan. They have been held responsible for bombings and violence in Tajikistan and Kyrgyzstan as the IMU has splintered into several groups. One of them, the Islamic Jihad Union (IJU), was deemed responsible for a series of attacks in Uzbekistan. What is more, it is alleged that they had planned Mumbai-style strikes in Europe.[24]

The appearance of jihadist groups has been linked to the dismal living conditions that the people of Central Asia must endure. According to a recent report of the International Crisis Group, all five Central Asian countries, with the possible exception of Kazakhstan, are on the verge of virtual collapse as viable political entities. Kyrgyzstan and Tajikistan are in the worst condition and may soon be deserving of the label "failed states." Turkmenistan and Uzbekistan are close behind them. But even Kazakhstan, where the regime of Nursultan Nazarbayev has access to vast energy wealth, faces a host of economic, political, and social problems that are likely to fracture Kazakhstan after this leader passes from the political scene.

The factors contributing to this dismal appraisal include aging leaders — like Karimov and Nazarbayev, who are in their early 70s — who have little legitimacy and have no one to succeed them; deteriorating infrastructures; declining health care systems; outmoded transportation networks; and hydroelectric and factory equipment that was constructed under Soviet rule and today is in advanced stages of disrepair. What is more, all face a human resource crisis as geriatric administrators and experts in a variety of fields are reaching retirement without qualified personnel to replace them. On the ecological front, Central Asia is encountering severe climatic strains, inciting water disputes among the disparate countries. Finally, the entire region is challenged by growing economic inequality and political polarization. Together, such unsettling problems are causing the emigration of society's most able contributors.

The specter of failed states worries not only Russian strategists, their American counterparts also are concerned about stability in the region. As the U.S. profile in Afghanistan diminishes, Central Asia will acquire greater significance. James Clapper, the Director of National Intelligence, has observed, "As the U.S. increases reliance on Central Asia to support operations in Afghanistan, the region's political and social stability is becoming more important."[25] As the U.S. withdrawal accelerates and troops and equipment are withdrawn from Afghanistan through the NDN, Central Asia will become a vital backstop for those U.S. forces that remain in the region.

Of course, it remains to be seen just how close the American-Russian partnership will remain. Skeptics in Washington will counsel against it as they do when joint-ventures of this nature are discussed, and hardliners in the Kremlin are certain to lobby against Russia joining the United States in military joint-ventures in what many still deem "their territory."

There may be some dispute over how to characterize the threat that Russia faces in the North Caucasus—an insurgency on the part of non-Russian peoples who seek their independence or Islamic terrorists who have openly declared their allegiance to al-Qaeda and to Global Jihad.

After two wars in Chechnya and rising violence in Ingushetia, Dagestan, and Kabardino-Balkaria, the region has become a major security headache for the Kremlin. In spite of a spate of economic, military, and political initiatives, the security situation in the North Caucasus remains dire, and expectations are that it will get worse and not better. The assassination of public officials is on the rise, along with attacks upon military bases and police stations, and the deaths involved have been on the upswing in spite of government attempts to crush the insurgents. At the same time, violence from this region has bled into Russia proper, as recent attacks on St. Petersburg and Moscow have revealed.

Although subject to debate, many Russian analysts see the growing popularity of radical Islam as the most important new element in explaining the intensity of the fighting in the North Caucasus. Among other things, Sayyid Qutb's writings are widely circulated and discussed by Islamic radicals there. Also, some of the insurgents have fought in Iraq, Afghanistan, and other jihadist struggles. It is noteworthy that members of radical Central Asian jihadist movements, such as Hizb ut-Tahrir and the Islamic Movement of Uzbekistan, have sought to proselytize in southern Russia. Given cultural and ethnic differences, however, they have not been hugely successful. Given the fact that about 20 percent of Russia's population is of the Islamic faith, the Kremlin will remain uneasy about any effort to turn them against Moscow.

Outside analysts correctly remark that Russia must address the growing violent upheaval in the region by using a variety of assets, not just military ones. This means addressing the socio-economic problems that underpin upheaval in the North Caucasus such as corruption, economic inequality, poverty, and widespread alienation among a public that complains that Moscow has treated the locals with contempt. But economic and social complaints aside, many of the insurgents are inspired by jihad, and they cannot be placated by promises of economic prosperity. Those who have chosen to be suicide bombers are not blowing themselves to oblivion because they want better kitchen appliances. They are fighting for a cause in which they are deeply committed, and they will press for its success unless they are crushed in battle. This is the response of Russian commanders when they are urged to seek reconciliation with the jihadists. On this matter, they reflect the convictions of American critics of COIN who have been urging U.S. military planners to acknowledge this disconcerting fact and to take appropriate forcible actions.[26]

The West cannot be of much help regarding a civil war within Russia, but the Kremlin has responded favorably to the U.S. Government's decision to include Doku Umarov, the region's leading jihadist, on its list of terrorists. Indeed, going so far as to put a $5 million bounty on his head has been met with approval among Russians who customarily warn about American power.[27] At the same time, ethnic insurgents, by associating themselves with Islamic jihadists, have compromised their movements in the eyes of Americans and European who otherwise might have supported their demands for greater independence from Moscow. David Kilcullen has observed, "The use of Chechnya as a terrorist haven during its period of self-rule compromised — perhaps fatally — the Chechen separatist cause, which is now seen largely as a cover for Islamist terrorist activity."[28] This, however, is not necessarily the opinion of those in the United States, who believe the source of the problem in the North Caucasus is Russian imperialism and not anti-Russian terrorism.

ENDNOTES - CHAPTER 6

1. *U.S. National Security Strategy*, Washington, DC: The White House, May 2010, p. 44.

2. Henry Kissinger and George Shultz, "Building on Common Ground with Russia," *Washington Post*, October 8, 2008.

3, Zbigniew Brzezinski, "From Poland's Tragedy, Hope for Better Ties with Russia," *TimeCNNWorld*, April 19, 2010.

4. Bob Woodward, *Bush at War*, New York, Free Press, 2002, p. 103.

5. *Ibid.*, p. 118.

6. In March 2011 when the United States and a coalition of the willing sought to stop Colonel Muammar Quaddafi from slaughtering his citizens, many American observers cited Russia's abstention as a defeat for reset. But that conclusion ignores a trenchant fact: by abstaining, Russia made it more difficult for China to veto the move. Here, then, was a partial victory for reset.

7. The airstrip that the Uzbeks made available could serve only the C-17 transport, not the larger C-5. Woodward, p. 178.

8. "Russia Not to Send Personnel to Afghanistan-Envoy," *Itar-Tass*, November 18, 2010.

9. Patrick F. P. Nopens, "Countering Afghan narcotics: a litmus test for effective NATO and Russian cooperation?" *Security Policy Brief*, No. 14, September 2010, Brussels, Belgium, EGMONT Institute, Royal Institute for International Relations, p. 2.

10. Russians, in response, cite the huge profits, corruption, and political cowardice that account for legal American arms merchants providing the Mexican mafia with weapons that have killed thousands of innocent people in that country, and a growing number in the United States as well.

11. Nopens, p. 6.

12. Mark Thompson, "Obama Loses a Key Base for Afghanistan," *Time Magazine*, February 19, 2009. See also Bill Gertz, "Inside the Ring: China in Kyrgyzstan," *Washington Times*, February 12, 2010.

13. *Cable Viewer and the Bug Pit/EurasiaNet.Org.*, February 5, 2011.

14. John C. K. Daly, "Are ISAF's Tenuous Supply Lines Sustainable?" Integrated Supply Network (ISN), March 2, 2011.

15. Steve Geary, "Northern Distribution Network to Shore up Afghan Supply Chain," New Breed Logistics: DC Velocity, June 28, 2010.

16. *Ibid.*, p. 1.

17. *Ibid.*, p. 2.

18. Daly.

19. Geary, p. 3.

20. Muhammad Tahir, "Central Asia Stands to Gain As NATO Shifts Supply Lines Away From Pakistan," RFE/RL, March 22, 2011. See also "Northern Distribution Network Keeps Growing," *eurasianet.org*, November 17, 2010.

21. Stephen Fidler and Gregory L. White, "Moscow Expands NATO's Routes," *Wall Street Journal*, November 18, 2010. For a more recent assessment of NDN, see Craig Whitlock, "For U.S., detours in supplying war effort," *Washington Post*, July 3, 2011.

22. Russian strategists also are concerned about China's penetration of the region. In public, the Russians speak favorably about Sino-Russian relations and taunt their American counterparts with the threat that Washington will have to face a powerful Russian-Chinese tandem in Central Asia and the Far East. In private, they concede that sharing a border exceeding 1,000 miles with a country whose population is 10 times their size is a daunting prospect. Also, in commenting upon Central Asia, Dmitri Trenin and Alexey Malashenko have observed: "Russia fears a rise in Islamic radicalism across the region and a revival of rebel activity in Uzbekistan and Kyrgyzstan. It does not have sufficient confidence in the solidity of the Central Asian regimes or in its own capacity to insulate the region from the influence of a victorious Taliban," p. 1.

23. Ahmed Rashid, p. 44.

24. Abubakar Siddique, "IMU's Evolution Branches Back to Central Asia," RFE-RL, December 6, 2010.

25. "Tajiskistan: The changing Insurgent Threats," *Asia Report No. 205-24*, Washington, DC: International Crisis Group, May 2011, pp. 9-10.

26. See, for example, Bing West, *The Wrong War: Grit, Strategy, and the Way Out of Afghanistan*, New York: Random House, 2011.

27. Sergey Markedonov, "Radical Islam in the North Caucasus," Washington, DC: Center for Strategic and International Studies, November 2010. In the spring of 2011, however, the Russian security forces had great success in killing many high value terrorists in the North Caucasus.

28. Lieutenant Colonel David Kilcullen, *Countering Global Insurgency*, Newport, RI: Naval War College, November 30, 2004, p. 7.

CHAPTER 7

CONCLUDING REMARKS AND RECOMMENDATIONS

Dramatic changes are unfolding in the international security environment that will have a profound impact upon the future of U.S. policies in Afghanistan and the Greater Middle East. They likewise will determine the nature of U.S.-Russian cooperation in Afghanistan and the surrounding region.

IDENTIFYING THE ENEMY: A CIVIL WAR WITHIN ISLAM

In an attempt to justify the invasion of Iraq, the military capacity of the September 11, 2001 (9/11) jihadists was grossly exaggerated. In the process, one of the fundamental principles of warfare was violated — "Know thine enemy!"

Al-Qaeda and affiliated jihadist movements have committed heinous terrorist acts in many areas of the world, and in the process have killed thousands of people. In that respect, they represent a global threat, but their capacity to achieve a 21st century Caliphate is beyond their reach. It is an absurdity to compare them with 20th century totalitarian movements. Adolph Hitler and Joseph Stalin possessed massive military war machines responsible for the death of tens of millions of people and physical destruction of seismic proportions. Vast numbers of heavily armed general purpose forces were required to crush fascism and to meet the threat of Soviet communism. A much smaller force is required to neutralize the jihadists whose principal weapon is terrorism. To confront them with a larger force only plays into their hands.

A more appropriate description of the turmoil roiling within Islam today is "civil war." The world witnessed something similar in August 1914. Then European civilization was stricken by a monumental eruption when the forces of the old and new order clashed within societies fractured by capitalism, industrialization, science, secularism, and urbanization. In this century, much the same thing is happening within the Islamic Umma as over one billion people struggle to strike a balance between traditional, religious-bound impulses and the dynamics of a modern secularized world.

While the fanciful campaign to create a 21st century Caliphate through brutal acts of terrorism is one manifestation of the Islamic Civil War, a second component is manifested in cultural, economic, political, and religious dislocations collectively known as the "Arab Spring." At this point, the course of the popular uprisings is difficult to plot, even with Quaddafi's fall in Libya, but it prompts several important observations:

- The potential for protracted and widespread violence is exceedingly high, and the repercussions for the international community are monumental. To cite just one example, a major disruption in the flow of oil from the Arab-Persian Gulf region would devastate a global economy still recovering from the greatest recession since the Great Depression.
- Not all areas of the Greater Middle East are of the same strategic value, and the United States must be selective in projecting its power in this vast area of the world.
- Washington can no longer rely on autocrats as instruments of stability since the strategic envi-

ronment that has sustained them is disintegrating.

- The Arab Spring's future is uncertain, but unlike their former rulers, the newly empowered masses will oppose policies long favored by the United States. Among other things, the Arab street will demand that Washington adopt a more even-handed approach to the Palestinian-Israeli conflict; that U.S. bases be reduced in size or shutdown altogether; and that American leaders stop preaching the glories of democracy while supporting dictators.[1]

As a consequence of these developments, Washington cannot unilaterally deal with the mayhem that the Islamic civil war has unleashed, and this reality is the basis for what some commentators have called the "Obama Doctrine." It rests on the truism that the United States must enlist allies in multilateral responses to jihadist threats. It also means collaborating with countries that may not share our values but are pursuing common security interests.

Clearly, when the violence spills over into our society, we must respond with the appropriate force. But it is a fantasy to think that even the world's premier military power can decide the outcome of the Islamic civil war. At best, events can be influenced at the margins. At times, the most prudent policy may be to do nothing at all. Had we fought the "right war" in Afghanistan, rather than the "wrong one" in Iraq, Afghanistan today might not be a democracy, but the odds are good that it would be free of the Taliban, though still perhaps a troubled society.

MAKING ROOM FOR THE REST

Fareed Zakaria has observed that the United States will remain the world's premier power for many years, but it must make room "for the rest."[2] Henceforth, U.S. foreign policy must be in compliance with the dramatic shift in power that is transpiring from the West to the East. For example, the countries known by the acronym BRIC (Brazil, Russia, India, and China) are demanding a voice in international institutions (those that the United States helped establish in the last century) that is commensurate with their massive populations and surging economies.

Both China and India have populations exceeding one billion citizens, and rates of growth that are among the highest in the world; Brazil, with almost 200 million people, has a population larger than any country in Europe, and its economy is growing at warp speed; Russia has a population in decline, but it possesses abundant mineral and hydrocarbon wealth and vast territory. In addition to its membership in the UN Security Council, it is second only to the United States in the capacity to wage a nuclear war.[3]

Even countries closely aligned with the United States no longer will accept its policies carte blanche. Turkey has demonstrated both the will and capacity to be a major player in Eurasian affairs in general, and those that involve Islamic countries in particular. Ever since refusing to allow the Americans a pathway into Iraq in 2003, the Turks have indicated that the United States can no longer take them for granted. Today, Turkey and Brazil have been searching for a settlement to the Iranian nuclear crisis independent of Washington and both favor an independent Palestine through UN intervention.

Relations between India and the United States have improved immeasurably as testified by Washington's providing New Delhi with help on the nuclear front, but India's support for American policies cannot be taken for granted. In April 2011, when the Obama administration wanted to impose harsh sanctions upon Syria for its slaughter of peaceful demonstrators, India refused to endorse the action.

It is within this changing international landscape that the United States must revise its approaches to world affairs.

The American Malaise.

As the saying goes, "The American people no longer want their country to serve as the world's policemen, answering 911 calls from all corners of the globe." Since the American Dream is beyond the grasp of a significant number of our citizens, their primary concern is to achieve personal security.

An alarming number are unemployed, while the average worker receives a smaller paycheck today than his father did 30 years ago. As a consequence, home ownership and a college education for the kids are beyond the reach of tens of millions of Americans. What is more, those facing retirement must contemplate shrunken pensions or none at all.[4] To make matters still worse, tax hikes may be inevitable, while states and municipalities cut programs for young and old alike. In the face of growing economic inequality, it will become politically daunting for congressional candidates or presidential aspirants to justify U.S. projections of power globally, including interventions costing billions that have been the norm since the end of World War II.

Unlike the 2010 elections, foreign policy concerns will have a bearing on the outcome of the 2012 races as an expanding number of voters see a link between foreign intervention and their own economic plight. Opposition to the Afghan war includes Americans on the left and right, and members of Congress are receiving mail from constituents demanding justification for spending $1 million annually to keep an American soldier on the Afghan battlefield when their state reduces health care benefits, emasculates public unions, and raises taxes.

Even prominent conservatives now question the rationale for maintaining a massive defense budget when the country faces a $14 trillion debt burden. According to a spokesman for Senator Tom Colburn, there are ideological reasons for conservatives to curb defense outlays that exceed U.S. needs. "By subsidizing our allies' defense budgets, American taxpayers are essentially subsidizing France's 35-hour work-week and Western European socialism."[5] Meanwhile, his liberal opponents, including President Obama, are calling for nation-building "at home."

Since there will be no quick turn-around of our sagging economy, the American military must live with what has been unthinkable: significant reductions in the defense budget. Toward this end, U.S. military officials have doubled the size of the hit that DoD must take in most recent assessments. As of late July 2011, it was assumed that the defense budget would be reduced by $800 billion over the next 12 years. Several months prior to that time, the estimate was half that figure. At the same time, and in contrast to the past, the companion notion that the United States must reduce its presence abroad no longer faces staunch opposition from the Republican Party (GOP) and its adherents. For example, in 2004, most Americans identified as "conservative Republicans" said it was "best to be active in world affairs," but 7 years later that majority slipped to 39 percent.[6]

At the same time, foreign policy and military planners cannot be unmindful of serious fissures in our society that deny our political leaders a nation united around a common narrative. The social compact that emerged from the New Deal and provided the vast majority of Americans with a stake in our democratic polity and free market economy is in peril. A unified America defeated fascism during World War II and subverted European communism during the Cold War. Today, a significant segment of our citizens is questioning the loyalty of their fellow Americans, while disunity at home and dramatic changes abroad represent huge barriers that our leaders must negotiate if they are to forge a common foreign policy agenda. It is against this backdrop of dramatic shifts at home and abroad that the following recommendations bearing on the Afghanistan Question are provided.

Sticking to the 2014 Afghanistan Exit Schedule.

On July 22, 2011, President Obama addressed the American people and announced his plans for the much anticipated troop withdrawal. He said that 10,000 troops would return home by the end of the year and an additional 23,000 by the close of 2012. The next day Admiral Mullen and General Petraeus expressed concern that the announced pullout went too far but endorsed Obama's call when they conceded that as President he was preoccupied with a host of pressing matters, not only military ones.

Critics, however, attacked the decision from the left and right alike. In the first case, the pullout was deemed too slow; in the second, too fast. Still, many military observers were pleased since it essentially provided for two more combat seasons to squeeze the Taliban. Moreover, some noted that the draw-down could start with support and not combat troops. In the process, the jihadists who were suffering mounting casualties would find cause to negotiate a settlement with the allied "Core Group" — Afghanistan, the United States, and Pakistan.

Meanwhile, close observers of the Afghanistan Question agreed on four pivotal points.

1. Obama's announcement had supported the view of the public and many foreign policy analysts that there was ample reason to end America's longest war. The path ahead was strewn with barriers, but the cost of remaining in Afghanistan exceeded the rewards.

2. The Counterinsurgency (COIN) versus counterterrorism (CT) debate had been decided in favor of the latter, counterterrorism. According to Bing West:

> We can't afford $100 billion a year. We have been waging war with an ATM that has run out of cash. We must implement a strategy that matches our reduced means. Being poorer, we have to fight smarter. That means cutting back on the unsuccessful missions of population protection and democratic nation-building. The Pashtun population has refused to turn against the Taliban, and the unreliable Karzai, with dictatorial powers and 4 more years in office, has no intention of building a democracy. Our conventional battalions are exerting too much effort for too little return.[7]

Of far greater significance, Senator Richard Lugar, arguably the most respected voice on foreign policy in the U.S. Senate, noted that "it is exceedingly difficult to conclude that our vast expenditures in Afghanistan represent a rational allocation of our military and financial assets."[8]

These provocative comments were in keeping with observations of CT proponents that it took less than 30 Navy seals to accomplish the bin Laden kill mission. Through small-unit operations and drone strikes, the leadership ranks of both al-Qaeda and the Taliban had been decimated. To maintain a heavy force in Afghanistan was strategically unjustified and served the cause of those jihadists who welcomed a heavy U.S. military footprint in Afghanistan just as they cherished the presence of Soviet forces there decades ago.

Of course, COIN proponents could favorably cite the testimony of Secretary Clinton before the U.S. Senate Foreign Relations Committee. The day after Obama's announcement, she said that COIN successes had provided a launching pad for CT advances, but agreed that there was no military rationale for a large contingent of U.S. troops to remain in Afghanistan beyond the President's timetable.[9]

3. The time had come to transfer the job of security to the Afghans, and now Karzai had been put on notice that he could not procrastinate any longer — he had to prepare for that outcome. To maintain a significant number of U.S. combat forces beyond 2014 would only prolong the Afghans' dependency upon the coalition and delay what was required of them. In Michael Walker's words:

> Our men and women in uniform have performed heroically in Afghanistan, but it is now time for the ANA to be battle-tested on a large scale and to take the lead in fighting this war. Without major victories on the battlefield, and without seizing and holding battle

133

space, the ANA will never attain the confidence and
reliability it needs to be a viable force.[10]

4. The stakeholder states and the medley of international institutions that would play a crucial role
bringing a successful conclusion to the Afghanistan
Question were now alerted that the time had come to
make preparations for a post-U.S. Afghanistan.

PREPARING FOR BONN II

To negotiate a peaceful solution to the Afghanistan
Question and avoid a wider war in the region, the
United States must start planning for an international
initiative similar to the first Bonn gathering — Bonn II.
China, India, Iran, Saudi Arabia, and Russia all have
indicated that they fear the security consequences
should a U.S. withdrawal result in a new civil war in
Afghanistan — most of them see the return of the Taliban in a similar light. Washington, therefore, must not
waste any time in embarking upon what is clearly a
monumental diplomatic endeavor.

In the spring of 2011, the news media reported that
a diplomatic solution to the mayhem in Afghanistan
was in the works. A series of secret talks had been
conducted by Michael Steiner, Germany's former
special representative to Afghanistan and Pakistan.
His Afghan Taliban counterpart was Tayyab Agha,
a close associate of Mullah Omar. Mid-level U.S. officials were involved in the discussions that first began
in Qatar and then moved to Bonn. These negotiations
centered on a planned December 2011 meeting in that
city.[11]

Indications were that Indian and Pakistani officials — at the highest levels of their respective gov-

ernments—had been talking positively about a peace settlement. What is more, it was alleged that the talks had the full support of the Karzai government.

Some observers argued that battlefield successes resulting in heavy Taliban casualties, impatience with their Pakistani "minders," and bin Laden's death explained why they were prepared to sign a reconciliation accord that endorsed the Afghanistan constitution, denounced al-Qaeda, eschewed violence, and acknowledged the legitimacy of the Karzai government. The accounts also mentioned that the U.S. special representative to Afghanistan and Pakistan (Af/Pak), Mark Grossman, was involved in the enterprise. Other accounts indicated that the jihadists remained confident about their future prospects, and that perception had hardened their position. In anticipation of the December Bonn gathering, then, no deal was guaranteed.

According to *Der Spiegel*, "The current negotiations revolve around the question of how security and stability can be guaranteed after Western troops withdraw. The central issue is the possible establishment of permanent American military bases in the country, a development the Taliban fears and categorically rejects."[12]

This is not the place to assess the many difficult issues that must be resolved, but the following observations provide some background to assess the prospects for a successful outcome. By far the greatest barrier is the Taliban. Even analysts who welcome negotiations with them express doubts about their cooperation. They fear Obama's announcement has encouraged the jihadists to hang tough. After all, time is on their side. This prognosis, however, ignores a compelling fact: the individuals fighting U.S. soldiers in Afghanistan include a wide diversity of groups. First and foremost are those associated with Mullah Omar's Quetta Shura—or leadership council—that most analysts associate with the label, "Taliban." But there are others jihadists that operate independently of the Quetta Shura like the Haqqani network and Hekmatyar's Hizb-e Islami, along with tribal entities, criminal organizations, and freelance fighters motivated by nationalistic, personal, or religious motives. In the early months of 2011 reports surfaced that many of these groups did not march to a single drummer, and some were in violent conflict with one another. Just as the prospect of a U.S. exit has produced divisions in the Karzai camp, the same is holding true for the Taliban.

Assuming Washington encourages most, if not all, of the major stakeholders to join the Bonn II gathering, the disparate "Taliban" leaders must ask themselves whether or not they want to alienate such a powerful collection of countries. Consider, in this connection, those who really believe that they may find themselves once again in power. What are their prospects if they alienate potential donors who can provide them economic assistance, training, and diplomatic and political cover; or, conversely, can empower their enemies? Once some of their cohorts embrace the peace process, others will be under pressure to join them or run the risk of being left behind. In short, a broad-based diplomatic undertaking of this kind is a potential game changer that may compel even the most radical Taliban to join Bonn II.

As indicated earlier, the bottom line for Washington is that the Taliban must end the violence, eschew al-Qaeda, acknowledge the government in Kabul, and abide by the Afghanistan constitution. The Taliban, in turn, has a bottom line of its own, the most critical being that it will not negotiate a settlement until foreign troops leave the country. With this position in mind, we perceive the following pathways to successful negotiations:

- A cease-fire is arranged that may allow the Taliban to retain their arms, but they are obliged to abide by all of the coalition's conditions.
- In return, the U.S. and ISAF troops leave Pashtun-dominated areas running roughly from the south to the eastern part of the country — that is from Helmand to Kunar province. International peacekeepers from Turkey join government troops, Taliban fighters, and elements of the Pakistani army as a pacifying force.
- To the West and North, U.S. and ISAF forces provide security along with the Afghan army and local police militias.
- Kabul, free of combat troops excepting law enforcement units, is under government control, but the Taliban and international personnel will have headquarters there.
- Over the next several years, outstanding differences — e.g., over the status of minority groups, women, political representation, and military deployments — will be reconciled.
- Meanwhile, donor countries and international economic and humanitarian organizations will operate in a violence-free environment.
- These activities will take place under the auspices of the UN and operate through a consortium of stakeholder countries while the CORE body constitutes the governing council. Potential key players are China, India, Iran, Russia, the Central Asian countries, and Saudi Arabia. NATO and the European Union (EU) must also participate in the endeavor.
- Depending upon how quickly progress is made, further troop reductions may transpire. Conse-

quently, the number of U.S. troops scheduled to be withdrawn may be accelerated even prior to Obama's schedule.

Officials in the Obama administration are of the opinion that advances toward reconciliation will not occur until sometime late in 2011, that is, after the Taliban lick their wounds and take stock of a problematic future. Of course, if the Taliban refuse to participate, the Bonn II proceedings will continue without them.

One more point needs to be underlined: all of the countries that have a stake in the future of Afghanistan have the incentives and capacity to provide the developmental support that can help meet the economic requirements of the country. Another way to look at this is to see international developmental assistance as a replacement for the civilian components of COIN that the United States cannot provide.

PLAN B: PARTITION

With bin Laden's death, U.S. officials have spoken optimistically about including the Taliban in peace talks, but events may prove that forecast a nonstarter. The Taliban may reject the idea, and it is uncertain whether or not Karzai will support or reject the idea. In addition to his conflicting remarks on this matter, his own future is problematic since he cannot legally run for re-election. Then, too, there is uncertainty about Pakistan. If the major stakeholders accepted Washington's invitation, Islamabad would be hard pressed not to join them, but then again there are powerful forces in Pakistan that are pulling in disparate directions. Furthermore, a peace drive may begin and achieve some success, but down the road end in a new round of violence.

It is thus imperative that the U.S. military ponder how it would react to a range of plausible outcomes as the 2014 deadline approaches. One of the most plausible ones is what we have called Plan B, or partition. It may occur as a result of a number of events. For example, in the face of a Taliban return to power, Hazaras, Uzbeks, and Tajiks—joined by anti-Taliban Pashtuns—resort to armed resistance and re-create an entity similar to the Northern Alliance. As an alternative to the Taliban, they will have scant difficulty securing funding for their armed forces; India, Iran, Russia, and under some circumstances possibly China, not to mention the United States, will provide arms, equipment, and money to help them protect most of western and northern Afghanistan.

Another catalyst to partition may occur as a consequence of a campaign on the part of the Pashtuns on both sides of the Afghan-Pakistan border to create some kind of Pashtun state. Not much is said about this prospect since most analysts presumably deem it unlikely, but no one doubts that as the U.S. withdrawal gains steam, a great deal of turbulence will follow in its wake. Clearly, then, a host of unanticipated consequences may materialize.

Without probing further into this admittedly difficult and complex alternative, the U.S. military must seriously consider what role it would play were the partition of Afghanistan to materialize. Clearly, no-fly zones come to mind along with air support and air surveillance operations, as well as the creation of logistical corridors through Russia and Central Asia. Washington might conduct defensive military operations to prevent an invasion of the enclave in the North or offensive ones to achieve the same objective. High-value targets would become subject to limited drone strikes and kill-and-capture operations, both conducted with the explicit purpose—at the minimum—of sustaining the division between the Taliban and Afghans who cannot abide living under their rule.

Preparing for the Worst Case Scenario (Plan C): A Taliban Victory.

Partition assumes a limited Taliban conquest, but U.S. strategists cannot ignore the worst case scenario, a total jihadist victory. As long as U.S. forces are in the country that will not happen, but given the huge problems that any Afghanistan government will face after 2014, all of Afghanistan might fall under Taliban control. A Taliban take-over could assume either of two forms.

The first constitutes a Taliban government that adheres to a national and not a global jihadist vision; it imposes strict "Islamist" policies upon the nation but denies radical jihadists sanctuaries, and proscribes international terrorist strikes of its own making.

> Many Taliban leaders of the older generation are still potential partners for a negotiated settlement. They are not implacably opposed to the U.S. or the West in general but to specific actions or policies in Afghanistan. These figures now understand the position of the international community much better than they did before 2001. They are not seeking a return to the failed interactions between the Taliban and the international community of the 1990s. At present they still represent the movement.[13]

These are the words of two researchers who have spent the last several years observing and interacting with Taliban in Kandahar, and they are not alone in their prognosis.

The Taliban leaders cannot forget that it took about 6 years for them to consolidate power in Afghanistan but only 3 months to lose their Islamic emirate as a consequence of a shattering military defeat. It is doubtful that they want a similar outcome. Moreover, a Western analyst based in Kabul has observed, "Taliban leaders say their agenda is purely regional. Unlike al-Qaida, they don't want to establish an emirate in Washington."[14] What is more, to have any hope of creating a viable regime, they must rely upon friends such as Pakistan and Saudi Arabia who find global jihadist policies unacceptable, and they must reach an accommodation with powerful enemies like Russia, the United States, and, perhaps, Iran and China.

Although its harsh fundamentalist policies, such as the mistreatment of women, will not win it many friends, a Taliban government that confined its radical religious practices to Afghanistan might be acceptable to the international community. In the final analysis, the same may hold true of most Afghans who prefer peace to a new round of fighting. Those who cannot abide the Taliban will leave the country or perhaps operate as insurgents.

The same would not hold true were a Taliban government to emerge that provided training camps for terrorists and orchestrated strikes against the United States and its allies. In the event of that outcome, the United States would respond militarily, most likely in a manner consistent with counterterrorism and not COIN doctrine. In this connection, we should take to heart some of the observations of old warriors who have closely observed operations in Afghanistan and younger ones who have served there. Representing the first category, Bing West has observed:

We didn't have a war-fighting doctrine for defeating the Taliban. Instead, we had a counterinsurgency doctrine for nation building, much like the Peace Corps on a giant scale. The new counterinsurgency dogma confused the soldiers because it confused roles. . . . Colonels insisted on detailed briefings before a single patrol could conduct a night ambush. This self-imposed restraint allowed the Taliban to control both its casualties and the pace and place of the fighting.[15]

Press reports indicate that many young soldiers who have served in Afghanistan are of the same opinion, thus challenging some of the basic principles of COIN. Specifically, they are convinced that the time has come to reconsider the rules of engagement when fighting an enemy that will place civilians at risk as an integral part of their military doctrine. Of course, jihadists who engage in such practices violate the rules of war. Consequently, it may be immoral to ask our warriors to sacrifice their lives when confronting an enemy that has contempt for secular rules of war because they answer to a "higher authority." When our soldiers inadvertently kill civilians because insurgents use them as shields, such actions are consistent with just war theory; it is the enemy that is engaging in immoral acts.[16] Furthermore, COIN practitioners must keep in mind that, in some instances, killing the enemy is the road to success and not attempts to win the hearts and minds of people who consider any kind of cooperation with foreign soldiers to be evil. If commanders or their civil masters consider this course unacceptable, perhaps they should not deploy combat troops in the first place.

One final observation must be stressed as the United States prepares to leave Afghanistan. An infrastructure, overt and covert, must be arranged that will sustain counterterrorist operations should the need arise to employ it in some future timeframe. It would include a network of sleeper cells, kill-and-capture teams, and arrangements with tribal leaders ready to wage guerrilla warfare against oppressive jihadist authorities. It would include drones and other technology that no longer allows a small number of terrorists to challenge a world class military establishment without fear of retribution. Now a small number of American fighters without concern about collateral casualties can impose lethal costs upon the insurgents. Young boys mesmerized by religious fantasies may continue to engage in suicide bombings without fear of death, but their elders who are more considerate of their own mortality may think twice about ordering terrorist strikes when they are the target of proficient enemies thousands of miles from their assumed sanctuaries.

Confronting Pakistan.

With the successful campaign against bin Laden, the duplicity of Pakistan has become a hot topic even among casual foreign policy mavens. Pakistan's harboring of al-Qaeda and Taliban terrorists that are killing Americans has prompted demands from the public and some of the political elite to confront the Pakistani civilian and military authorities and demand that they hand over individuals who are associated with other terrorist organizations that have sanctuaries in the country. This would include Mullah Omar, Ayman Zawari, Saif al Adel, leaders in the Haqqani network, and the Lashkar-e-Tayyiba terrorist group that was responsible for the Mumbai atrocities. If the Pakistanis fail to comply, we should stop providing them the billions of dollars in economic and military aid that enables them to embrace the status quo.

Washington-based Pakistan experts strongly oppose such provocative actions, responding first, that in spite of Pakistan's duplicity, there is no positive outcome to the Afghanistan crisis without Pakistan's help. Second, they say we must accept business as usual with Islamabad because it is a nuclear power, and even if its nukes are under the safe control of the Army, no one can discount a nuclear show-down between India and Pakistan that would envelop the region and perhaps much of the world in a nuclear conflagration.

This view has strong advocates in both political parties, but as we approach the 2012 presidential election, it is clear that existing relations between Washington and Islamabad are in crisis and may no longer be sustainable. Growing numbers of Americans feel unprecedented economic pain, and they have begun to associate it with expensive foreign ventures like the wars in Iraq and Afghanistan. Consequently, it will be difficult for any President to maintain the existing level of economic and military aid to a country that is harboring terrorists killing Americans. What is more, when U.S. voters hear reports that the top military brass in Pakistan enjoy lucrative business enterprises or have access to funds that conceivably are part of the billion dollar aid package that is provided annually by American taxpayers, they are bound to raise hell. At the same time, Pakistan has been a major, perhaps the most significant, source of nuclear weapons proliferation in the world. Libya, Iran, and North Korea have been on the receiving end of help from the Pakistan scientific proliferator, A. Q. Khan.

Moreover, India and Pakistan must on their own resolve their disputes over Kashmir and other security-related issues. The United States cannot do so for them. In a word, both countries must adopt the same triad of measures that prevented a nuclear exchange between the United States and the USSR during the Cold War: deterrence; arms control; and crisis management. There has been progress of late on stabilizing the nuclear relationship between India and Pakistan, and the United States must do whatever it can to facilitate more harmonious relations between the two sides. Through Bonn II, they may find a way, with the support of the international community, to reduce their respective fears about an Afghan settlement.

In considering U.S.-Pakistani discord, Bruce Riedel takes the United States to task for not acknowledging the huge problems that confront both Pakistan's civilian and military leaders. He notes in particular that while the George W. Bush administration celebrated a commitment to democratization, it worked closely with General Pervez Musharraf, a military dictator. That act of hypocrisy did not sit well with many Pakistanis and contributed to anti-American resentments. He urges Washington to reinforce the civilian authorities in Islamabad, but at the same time he makes the case that the military really has the upper hand.

Furthermore, Riedel provides convincing evidence that the Pakistani military has been extremely reckless. For example, some members of the ISI encouraged attacks on Indian cities such as the Mumbai terrorist strike that killed 116 people. He also underscores that in an earlier attack on the parliament in New Delhi, high-level officials were deemed priority targets. The Pakistani officials who were complicit in such rash operations recklessly ignored the fact that they were provoking a country that defeated Pakistan in three wars and that possesses a nuclear arsenal equal to or even more potent than their own.

Yes, Indian-Pakistani enmity might be reduced if Washington helped resolve their differences over Kashmir, but given the refusal of either side to reconcile their differences regarding this conflict, does anyone really believe that United States has the capacity to help end it? The time has come to recognize that the United States can no longer hope to shape all international events.

On the basis of this evidence, U.S. leaders must ask themselves whether they can rely upon their partners in Pakistan to change their ways when they have indicated time and again that their pathological fear of India makes them not only an unreliable partner, but a dangerous one as well. Both the civilian and military leaders in Pakistan must be made to understand by their American counterparts that the status quo cannot endure, and that the time has come to develop a security partnership that is transparent, honest, and fruitful. In short, that means that no American President can allow Pakistan to support terrorists who are killing our soldiers, and that if this support does not end, there will be consequences, including a cut-off of funds to Pakistan's military establishment.[17]

Both the civilian and military leadership in Islamabad may ignore such threats for the reasons that have been cited: namely, that the Americans cannot hope to achieve success in Afghanistan without Pakistan and, should Washington punish it, the United States may destabilize Pakistan and foster a nuclear showdown with India. The Americans certainly do not want that to happen.

The Pakistani elite, however, cannot be unmindful of the growing anger on the part of the U.S. public when they hear that Pakistan is receiving billions of their hard-earned tax dollars while it refuses to deny sanctuaries to jihadists that are killing our young soldiers. What is more, many Americans are asking why we are arming a flaky ally that is using our military aid to threaten the world's largest democracy — India. Observations of this nature resonate across the U.S. political spectrum, and they will gain momentum in the tempest of the 2012 presidential campaign.

In sum, the future of U.S.-Pakistan relations looks bleak, but there is some hope that the anticipated Bonn II gathering — or a similar diplomatic initiative — will force them both to set aside their mutual points of conflict in favor of a more significant outcome — a negotiated settlement to the Afghanistan Question that may not please them on all counts but goes a long way toward promoting their most basic security concerns.

Before closing the books on Pakistan, it is imperative for the U.S. defense community to think about the unthinkable: the implosion of Pakistan. That outcome may be remote, but it would constitute a truly monumental threat to regional and perhaps world peace, and therefore should not be discounted. Most experts believe that in spite of its many problems — ecological, economic, ethnic, military, and political — Pakistan will endure. Perhaps, but there is mounting evidence to the contrary, and it would be a mistake to ignore it. Recall that not too long ago the Soviet Union arguably possessed far greater resources to prevent its demise, but nonetheless collapsed. Moreover, Pakistani experts say the army would not permit the state to collapse, but once again the Red Army and associated security services were robust but in the end proved incapable of preventing the Soviet Empire's implosion.

The Time Has Come to Reduce Our Profile in the Greater Middle East.

On February 25, 2011, Secretary Gates stunned a West Point audience: "In my opinion, any future defense secretary who advises the president to again send a big American land army into Asia or into the Middle East or Africa should have his head examined."[18] Implicit in the Secretary's words is the message that the time has come for the United Staes to reduce its profile in the Middle East, now roiled by the monumental confrontations between the old autocrats and the emerging middle class and the poverty-stricken masses.

Initially, it was assumed that the Arab Spring would promote reforms that resulted in democratic governments, more open social systems, and market-driven economies that would reduce the income inequality that is the hallmark of the Arab and Islamic world. But, alas, the struggle may last for years and produce widespread violence and the return to power of anti-democratic elements. In addition, the fate of U.S. allies like Iraq, Israel, Egypt, Jordan, and the Gulf sheikdoms, as well as those that are strategically vital to the future of the oil-rich region like Iran, Lebanon, and Syria, are all in question. The Arab Spring, then, may presage years of widespread turmoil and violence in a region where 70 percent of the world's petroleum is located.

Mindful of such further serious turmoil in the Arab-Iranian lands, and with diminishing assets itself, the United States must make a choice: to remain in Afghanistan and expand our involvement in Central Asia for many years, or to focus primarily on the strategically vital Arab-Iranian arena. Given the facts on the ground, it appears that doing both may be beyond Washington's capacity and its vital self-interest. Whatever choice it makes, the United States must urgently search for partners. Given the plight of the European project, that may mean reaching out to countries that have not been closely allied with it, such as China and Russia as well as the Central Asian autocracies. Critics who claim that a reset with such autocracies is unjustified must provide an answer to those who ask, "But what are the alternatives?" For example, should we refuse to accept Chinese investments in U.S. Government securities because of Beijing's less than stellar human rights record? Or should we refuse to accept pathways into Afghanistan through Uzbekistan because of Karimov's authoritarian rule?

Above all, in assesssing future military operations in the Greater Middle East, Pentagon planners should pay heed to Hamid Fhadil, a political scientist at Baghdad University who spoke in response to questions about why there was a spike in terrorist attacks in Iraq: "If the Americans leave, Al Qaeda will no longer have an excuse to operate throughout the country. Al Qaeda wants Americans to stay here so they will have Iraq as a battlefield to fight the Americans."[19]

Sustaining and Enlarging Security Cooperation with Russia.

U.S.-Russian security cooperation in Afghanistan has been limited but successful. By the end of 2011, more than 50 percent of the cargo to be delivered to coalition forces will travel by way of the NDN.[20] It will become an even more critical logistical asset as coalition forces begin to exit Afghanistan, and agreements with Central Asian and Russian authorities permit cargo heretofore prohibited — such as lethal equipment — to traverse their land and air space. In addition, help in the way of arms, intelligence, and training from the Russian side has facilitated the coalition's mission in Afghanistan.

Looking forward, expanding commercial relations between Russia and Afghanistan are on the upswing. On January 21, 2011, Karzai was the first Afghan president to visit Moscow since Najibullah did so in the late 1980s. He, along with a number of prominent Afghans, met with Medvedev and Putin to discuss wider economic cooperation. Yevgeny Primakov, the head of Russia's Chamber of Commerce, pointed to upgrading the Afghan infrastructure projects that were initially built during the Soviet era, such as a pre-fabricated housing factory, and one that produces cement in Jabal Siraj. Both would be funded by the Moscow Industrial Bank.

Karzai, in turn, cited a $500 million rise in bilateral trade and Afghanistan's interest in Russia's hydrocarbon assets. He also welcomed access to the technical expertise that his northern neighbor could provide, as well as military assistance such as the 20,000 AK-47 rifles Russia donated to his forces and its help in training 250 members of the Afghan police force.[21]

Since opening a trade office in Kabul in 2002, the Afghans have eagerly accommodated Russian commercial efforts that are associated with Soviet-era development programs like the Naglu hydroelectric station and "the Salang tunnel that links Kabul to the Northern provinces and was constructed by the Soviets."[22] Simultaneously, Russia is intent on connecting its pipelines and rail transit systems running through Central Asia to those in Afghanistan. As funding associated with extensive American military operations declines, Kabul will look to Russia as an eager economic partner.

On the diplomatic front, Russia through the UN can encourage stakeholders to fund economic and humanitarian programs that ease Afghanistan's economic challenges. Russia is in a position likewise to advance progress of the international effort to make Bonn II a success. It also enjoys close relations with China and India and can help encourage both of these emerging powers to endorse a diplomatic campaign to stabilize the entire region.

In event of partition, Russia's assistance to the Northern Alliance's success would be critical — most specifically in maintaining air and land corridors to it and providing arms, ammunition, and supplies required to sustain the non-Taliban entity. Simultaneously, were the worst-case scenario to materialize, the Tajik and Uzbek insurgents affiliated with the Taliban would become more aggressive throughout Central Asia. Under these circumstances, Russia might take active military measures to meet the jihadist threat. Fearful of their security, those Central Asian leaders that were wary of Russian soldiers operating on their territory might actually welcome them.

In the face of a range of plausible scenarios, the American defense community must assess the feasibility of joint U.S.-Russian military operations. But a broad range of concomitant questions must also be addressed. What are the prospects of joint military cooperation in meeting a resumed jihadist threat in Afghanistan or Central Asia? What would be the character of this military cooperation? Are joint combat operations even plausible, given existing reservations in both Washington and Moscow about the good will of the other side? And if they are plausible, what about the command structure and from which venue would they operate? Finally, what are the prospects of China joining Russia and the United States in a range of efforts to develop and stabilize Afghanistan, or, barring that, at least Beijing standing aside and not interfering in those efforts?[23]

Critics of the reset in both Washington and Moscow, however, have been unrelenting in derogating the reset campaign. But in addition to the sanguine prospects engendered by the New START, U.S. critics of the reset overlook the fact that Russia joined the Americans and Europeans in sanctioning Tehran for failing to comply with UN resolutions regarding its drive for nukes. Likewise, Moscow withheld an arms sale that amounted to close to a billion dollars. True, the Kremlin often uses harsh language in criticizing Western foreign policy initiatives, but in the final analysis, it rarely backs its caustic words with punishing actions. Russia needs the reset, and this conviction encouraged Medvedev in the May 2011 G-8 gathering in France to call for Quaddafi's expulsion from office. This was a significant setback for the Libyan dictator since he had cited his "close" relationship with Moscow as evidence that he was not a pariah in the eyes of the international community.

Of course, Russian critics assert that, aside from the American pledge to provide a $5 million reward for information leading to the arrest of the North Caucasus terrorist, Umarov, Russia has not gotten much in return for the reset. That is categorically untrue, since coalition troops have suffered the loss of considerable blood and treasure in Afghanistan — in the case of the United States, about 1,600 deaths — in order to crush the very same jihadists that deem Russia an enemy of Islam.

One can make the case that ongoing reset initiatives collectively amount to an expanding network of crisis managers, freelance defense analysts, political leaders, and key policymakers in both camps who are breaking down barriers to cooperation. They are creating a common partnership culture that reminds one of the U.S.-Soviet networks of individuals and organizations that thrived during the "Golden Age of Arms Control." For decades, it served as an educational as well as a confidence-building mechanism and helped prevent the military showdown that haunted leaders in both countries. It operated at a time when the participants saw the other as a dangerous and authentic security threat. Today, no one in either camp — with some rare exceptions — really believes that an American-Russian nuclear exchange is plausible.

These positive events aside, there are serious roadblocks to expanding joint-security ventures.[24] For example, as long as concerns about another Russian-Georgian war exist and the future of South Ossetia and Abkhazia are unsettled, many in the West will reject further cooperation with Moscow. Charges that Russia is interfering with the prospects for democracy in Belarus are not winning it friends in the West, either. What is more, by exploiting its energy wealth to manipulate its former Baltic republics and East European satellites, Moscow is compromising the prospects for reset. Perhaps the most toxic disagreement involves the U.S. missile defense system that will be deployed in Europe. Some analysts believe that it will undermine the reset since Washington simply cannot allow Moscow to have a real voice in how the system operates. That conclusion may prove erroneous since it appears that the Obama administration truly wants to reach some kind of agreement with Russia on this matter.

Notwithstanding the positive signs, U.S. analysts cannot be unmindful that Russia's capacity for joint-security operations is limited. In addition to a shrinking population, Russian society is stricken by corruption, lawlessness, a dangerous over-dependency upon its hydrocarbon wealth, and a track record of failed military reform. The Kremlin overlords continue to demand they be treated as equals, but by any measuring stick available — demographic, economic, military, and political — Russia is hardly equal to the United States, much less to the combined strength of the EU, Japan, and South Korea. This is not meant to diminish Russia or its people, but rather to hearken to Putin's advice that officials in Washington and Moscow must cooperate on the basis of common interests rooted in reality. In this connection, some in the West warn that Russia has a grand strategy, but the Americans and Europeans do not have a similar agenda. But that is not the problem here. Rather, it is that Russia has international ambitions that exceed its capabilities, and that disconnect could undermine the reset.

In the final analysis, the reset may fail, but in its 2011 statement on combating terrorism, the United States emphasized as a core principle the need to find international partners in the fight against terrorists.[25] Even if there is successful closure to the Afghanistan Question, al-Qaeda and like-minded jihadist groups will continue to operate elsewhere — Yemen, Somalia, or some other majority Islamic country where the government is weak and society is in turmoil. Indeed, they may launch terrorist attacks from somewhere in Europe, including Russia, or even the United States. In most of these cases, joint efforts to fight jihadist terrorism make sense, even if the payoff is modest.

On the basis of American-Russian cooperation in Afghanistan, Washington should persist in joint-security cooperation with Moscow. If there is concrete evidence that the partnership is no longer viable, then it is appropriate to shut it down—but not until that point is reached. In keeping with the principles of prudent internationalism, all opportunities for multilateral cooperation that safeguard the United States should be welcomed.

ENDNOTES - CHAPTER 7

1. For an early assessment of the Arab Spring, see the series of articles published under the rubric "The New Arab Revolt," in the May/June 2011 issue of *Foreign Affairs*.

2. Fareed Zakaria, *The Post American World*, New York: W. W. Norton & Co., May 2008.

3. For a Chinese commentary on BRIC (Brazil, Russia, India, and China), see Wang Xiaotian, "BRICS target economic reform," *China Watch, The China Daily*, May 6, 2011.

4. Joseph Stiglitz, the Noble Prize winner in economics, forecasts slow economic growth and high rates of unemployment for many years, and in this forecast he is joined by economists of all schools of thought. See his "Alternatives to Austerity," Project Syndicate, December 6, 2010.

5. Carrie Budoff-Brown, "Will New War Nix Big Defense Cuts?" *Politico*, March 28, 2011.

6. See Craig Whitlock, "Pentagon girds for deeper cuts," *Washington Post*, July 21, 2011; and "More Conservatives Say 'Come Home, America'," Washington, DC: Pew Research Center Publications, June 16, 2011.

7. Bing West, *The Wrong War*, New York: Random House, 2011, p. 252. Colonel Gian Gentile is in agreement with this prognosis: "American strategy in Afghanistan currently suffers from a

dysfunctional mismatch between the heavy amount of resources committed through a long-term campaign of nation building and President Barack Obama's reasonably limited core political goal in the region to 'disrupt, disable, and defeat' al-Qaeda." See his "The 'Condition-Based' Afghan Loophole," Washington, DC: Council on Foreign Relations, online publication, December 10, 2010.

8. David A. Fahrenthold and Paul Kane, "On Hill, Renewed Calls for Rapid Afghan Pullout," *Washington Post*, May 11, 2011. A number of GOP presidential aspirants also have called for a U.S. pull-out from Afghanistan, and their cohorts in Congress indicate that economic prudence favors that outcome as well.

9. Hilary Rodham Clinton, Secretary of State, Testimony before the Senate Foreign Relations Committee, U.S. Department of State, June 23, 2011.

10. Michael F. Walker, "The Afghan Army Needs to Fight," *Washington Post*, May 1, 2011.

11. Among the press reports treating peace talks, see Mark Landler and Helene Cooper, "Qaeda Woes Fuel Talk of Speeding Afghan Pullback,"*New York Times*, June 2011; David Ignatius, "Signs of an Afghan Deal," *Washington Post*, May 26, 2011. For a comprehensive discussion of a peace plan, see Lakhdar Brahimi and Thomas R. Pickering, Task Force Co-Chairs, *Afghanistan: Negotiating Peace*, New York: The Century Foundation Press, 2011.

12. Susanne Koelbl and Holger Stark, "Germany Mediates Secret U.S. Taliban Talks," *Spiegel Online*, May 24, 2011.

13. Alex van Linschoten and Felix Kuehn, *Separating the Taliban from Al-Qaeda: The Core of Success in Afghanistan*, New York: Center on International Cooperation, February 2011.

14. These are the words of Thomas Ruttig at the Afghanistan Analysts Network. See Koelbl and Stark.

15. West, p. 111.

16. For a discussion of just war theory, see Richard J. Krickus, "On The Morality of Chemical/Biological Warfare," *The Journal of Conflict Resolution*, Vol. 9, No. 2, 1965, pp. 200-210.

17. For a discussion of U.S.-Pakistani relations by a seasoned American official, see Bruce Riedel, *Deadly Embrace*, Washington, DC: The Brookings Institution, 2011.

18. George Friedman, "Never Fight a Land War in Asia," STRATFOR, May 1, 2011.

19. See Michael S. Schmidt, "Threat Resurgence in Deadliest Day of Year for Iraq," *New York Times*, August 15, 2011.

20. Whitlock.

21. Aunohita Mojumdar, "Karzai Visits Moscow as Russia Eyes Greater Role in Afghanistan," *The Christian Science Monitor*, January 20, 2011; Owen Matthews and Anna Nemtsova, "Back To Afghanistan," *Newsweek*, November 3, 2010.

22. Marlene Laurelle, *Beyond the Afghan Trauma: Russia's Return to Afghanistan*, Washington, DC: The Jamestown Foundation, August 2009, p. 19.

23. Russian and Chinese troops have participated in joint military exercises, and together they can field a military force capable of engaging jihadists. It remains to be seen, however, whether such a force is feasible, given a relationship that has been marked by old grievances and current suspicions. Will they use the SRO as an instrument for anti-jihadist military operations? And how will they interact with the United States? U.S. military planners must give serious consideration to all of these questions in exploring the reset's future, even though at present the prospects of China's playing a positive role in stabilizing Afghanistan appear slim. Given its extensive and growing commercial interest in Afghanistan, however, stability in that country is in Beijing's vital interest. This realization may ultimately convince it that cooperation with Washington on this matter is prudent. Up to the present time, China has been a free-rider, and its projects in Afghanistan have been protected by the American-led coalition. But while it has characterized U.S. troops in the region as threatening, like

Moscow, it has expressed concern about the future of Afghanistan after the Americans leave. Meetings between American and Chinese officials in Washington in the spring of 2011 have been characterized by Obama administration officials as "ground-breaking."

24. Looking forward to future reset prospects, most seasoned observers are cautious in their assessments. Dmitri Trenin sees Russian help in Afghanistan as limited and tactical and does not presage extensive American-Russian security cooperation. "Despite some tactical collaboration in Afghanistan, there is virtually no potential for serious cooperation between Russia and the United States on Central Asia." Still, he sees Russia's interest in a reset with the United States as part of a broader strategy of achieving good relations with the West to help jump-start Russia's modernization program. Dmitri Trenin, "Contemporary Issues in International Security: Central Asia," Stephen J. Blank, ed., *Central Asian Security Trends: Views From Europe And Russia*, Carlisle, PA: Strategic Studies Institute, U.S. Army War College, April 2011, p. 72.

25. See *National Strategy For Counterterrorism*, Washington, DC: The White House, June 2011. In considering the issue of partners, it is evident that, unlike the European countries, Russia has compelling reasons to join the United States in enhancing Afghanistan's security. For most Europeans living in the Western part of the Continent, they see no serious existing threat associated with Afghanistan and lament that their American allies are now obsessed with a new cold war, only it is manifested in turmoil afflicting the Islamic world. This explains why ever since 9/11, Europe's defense outlays have plunged 15 percent, prompting Secretary Gates to complain about the Europeans' failure to carry their fair share of the defense burden. As a consequence, he warned, "The blunt reality is that there will be dwindling appetite and patience in the U.S. Congress—and in the American body politic writ large—to expend increasingly precious funds on behalf of nations that are apparently unwilling to devote the necessary resources or make the necessary changes to be serious and capable partners in their own defense." See Transcript of Defense Secretary Gates' Speech on NATO's Future, *Wall Street Journal*, June 10, 2011, available from *WSJ.com*. These words do not resonate since most ordinary Europeans do not care if the United

States reduces its defense budget as personal security is their major concern; that is, security imperiled by national economic difficulties that are a by-product of a massive display of corruption and ineptness on the part of their American cousins. That is the colossal scam hatched by Wall Street sharpies who exploited the dream of home ownership to devastate the U.S. and eventually the global financial system. Likewise, the specter of the European Project fragmenting into disparate political and economic entities and the collapse of the Euro zone is their major "security" nightmare.

U.S. ARMY WAR COLLEGE

Major General Gregg F. Martin
Commandant

*****

STRATEGIC STUDIES INSTITUTE

Director
Professor Douglas C. Lovelace, Jr.

Director of Research
Dr. Antulio J. Echevarria II

Author
Dr. Richard J. Krickus

Director of Publications
Dr. James G. Pierce

Publications Assistant
Ms. Rita A. Rummel

*****

Composition
Mrs. Jennifer E. Nevil

www.ingramcontent.com/pod-product-compliance
Lightning Source LLC
Chambersburg PA
CBHW080017280326
41934CB00015B/3375